Breathe well.
Live well.
namaste,
Sharon ♡

Learning To Breathe, Learning To Live

Simple Tools To Relieve Stress And Invigorate Your Life

Sharon Harvey Alexander

Balboa Press books may be ordered through booksellers or by contacting:

Balboa Press
A Division of Hay House
1663 Liberty Drive
Bloomington, IN 47403
www.balboapress.com
1 (877) 407-4847

Print information available on the last page.

ISBN: 978-1-5043-8413-1 (sc)
ISBN: 978-1-5043-8415-5 (hc)
ISBN: 978-1-5043-8414-8 (e)

Library of Congress Control Number: 2017910849

Balboa Press rev. date: 08/14/2017

Dedication

With appreciation and an eternal flow of loving energy
I dedicate this book to my children,
Sarah and Taylor Alexander.

You have been my greatest teachers.

Thank you for sharing this lifetime with me
and for good-naturedly rolling your eyes
every time I've suggested that you:

Remember to Breathe!

PRAISE FOR *LEARNING TO BREATHE, LEARNING TO LIVE*

The solutions to life's challenges are utterly simple, obvious, undeniable, and accessible. Yet we miss them, distracted by the demands and drama of work, relationships, illness, hobbies, ego, and emotions. *Learning to Breathe, Learning to Live* is a gift to help reduce stress and bring focus back to the Self, wherein lie the answers we seek. I owe Sharon a big thank you for a book that helped bring me back in tune with the answers within me.

Steve Bauhs,

Renewable Energy Aficionado and Yoga Neophyte

As a first-line healthcare provider working in a busy Urgent Care department, I routinely care for patients with high stress and anxiety levels who are desperate for relief. The best medicine is deep breathing. Breathing is available, free and non-habit forming! Effective breathing is something each of us needs to practice in order to use it effectively. Learn to do that by reading this book. Sharon Harvey Alexander offers step-by-step instructions to guide people of all ages and abilities to a healthier place. She takes us through the mechanics of breathing for relaxation, and then builds on that foundation with thoughtful and effective practices that build upon each other. Pick up a copy. Spend time with the practices in it. You may find your own levels of stress diminish as you pay attention to how you breathe. Take the reins of your health care and guide yourself to a better feeling place. Why not begin today? Learn to breathe, and feel better physically, mentally, and emotionally too.

Claudia Williams, Physician's Assistant,
Longmont United Hospital, Emergency Care

Sharon has given us a simple yet profound book. The daily stress we all experience is alleviated by the basic practices described here. The subtle stress reduction methods included in this book reduce feelings of chaos and guide us back to the source of our true selves. And there's plenty of background information to placate the inquiring mind. Try this book. Receive the benefits of these practices. You will be happy you did!

Kenton Bloom, Owner/Manager,
Many Rivers Healing Arts and Movement Studio

After reading *Learning to Breathe, Learning to Live* as I lay on my couch on the weekends, I started breathing deeply for a few minutes each day. I love how that relaxes and realigns me. It helps me shift my focus from the stressful to the satisfying parts of my productive lifestyle.

Jen Greene, Business Director, YES Energy

It was easy to relax in my chair as I considered the material in this book. I felt better, too, as I brought awareness to my breath. The practices are easy to implement and there's something for everyone here.

David Ballard,

retired Architect for the National Park Service

Table Of Contents

FOREWORD

I have had the pleasure of knowing and teaching with yoga therapist and stress management educator Sharon Harvey Alexander in her beautiful private studio in Boulder, Colorado, for the past several years. Sharon creates a safe and inviting space for many to experience her fine teachings, which include mindful movement practices, therapeutic yoga applications, and her exquisite work with the breath. Her kind attention to comfort and thoughtful ways of expressing her knowledge bring many to her doorstep.

In *Learning to Breathe, Learning to Live*, Sharon artfully shares her experiences in guiding and healing with breath work, while at the same time, giving the reader simple yet profound tools necessary to help themselves through *pranayama* (Sanskrit for life force/breath work), which she creatively calls an art form. She reveals how to breathe with awareness to aid anyone and everyone in releasing stress, thus allowing them to feel better and enabling them to enjoy life more fully. With discipline and practice, one can find expression, refinement, and joy—the very meaning of art.

From the Easy Breath and Belly Breathing Practices and the other techniques included in this book, the reader is taken through detailed steps to encourage his or her own experience. I found myself practicing as I read, and the benefits were immediate.

As an anatomist, kinesiologist, and author of movement science books, I appreciate Ms. Alexander's references to both the mechanics of breath and how it calms the central nervous system. In writing The *Vital Psoas Muscle*, I refer to the relation of the diaphragm and the psoas major through myofascial tissue and how this connection enhances and relaxes the central nervous system. Sharon presents this in an understandable and user-friendly way, permitting the reader to follow breath work descriptions easily without getting too bogged down in scientific terminology.

I especially enjoy the wisdom insights found throughout the

book. Referencing traditional practices from long ago supports the reader in connecting to the present as well. The historical perspective is important and meaningful.

Ms. Alexander has written an in-depth yet easy-to-follow book that I feel readers will find useful and enjoyable.

Jo Ann Staugaard Jones,

Author of *The Concise Book of Yoga Anatomy*, *The Vital Psoas Muscle*, and *The Anatomy of Exercise and Movement*, and international educator (www.Move-Live.com)

PREFACE

It was a cold, dark winter evening when a reserved, older man shuffled into one of my breathing classes, accompanied by his wife of many years. She had signed them up for the class, hoping to find tools to alleviate her husband's physical struggles. He extended his hand in timid introduction. Behind the man trailed an oxygen machine to which he was attached via long, slender tubes. His wife anxiously reported that it was difficult for her husband to keep his oxygen levels up and that as a consequence, work had become a challenge, as had sleep.

With no idea about what to expect from the class, she told me that he had taken an oxygen reading in the car before coming in, and his level was eighty-four percent. This reading was consistent with his levels on most days.

At the end of the class, he privately measured his oxygen

level again while I visited with others. With a smile on his face and relief painted across his wife's face, he told me that his level was ninety-eight percent, perhaps the highest to be expected when breathing from a machine. This was a beautiful example of what is possible when we learn to pay attention to how we breathe.

As a breath coach, certified holistic stress management educator, and professional yoga therapist, I support individuals and groups in reclaiming a sense of wholeness and well-being by teaching them how to breathe well and put trust in their inner compass. I know through experience that proper breathing is the foundation of all successful stress management programs. Effective breathing is essential if you want to live a long and vibrant life. The six simple, yet profound techniques and two guided visualizations in this book are meant to help you establish that foundation.

It is my sincerest hope that the material in this book will benefit millions of people around the world as they seek to discover, reclaim, and/or maintain a vital and satisfying life. If you want to improve your work life, enhance your relationships, or simply take better care of yourself, refining how you breathe would be a great first step.

It may seem ironic that we must attend a class or read a book to learn how to breathe. Yet many of us barely give breathing much thought as our attention moves through the obligations of the day, which include work, relationships, finances, and hobbies. Thankfully, our breathing continues automatically, bringing oxygen to the cells in our tissues and removing waste. At the same time, breathing is a function we can manipulate. When we do so, we often experience a beneficial change.

By learning to pay attention to our breathing, we may enhance the functioning and efficiency of other body systems as well, including the nervous system, the immune system, the digestive system, the reproductive system, and the circulatory system. By dedicating only a few minutes each day to paying attention to how we breathe, stress and strain begin to melt away. We feel better almost immediately. Offering this conscious support to the breath allows it to do its job more effectively. The techniques in this book will help you feel better tomorrow than you do today— even if you're not breathing from an oxygen machine.

Whether young or old, fit or weak, male or female, learning how to breathe helps you learn how to live. No matter how busy you are, or what stage of life you're in, there's no better time to tune in to the rhythms of life that are reflected through your breath and no better time to visualize the quality of life that you desire.

INTRODUCTION

I offer this book in the hope that it will support you in cultivating a joyful, steady, and productive life even when living in what may be tumultuous times. It is not only a guidebook, but also a book about how to be the best person you can be. Please take your time to enjoy it. It only takes a few minutes a day to explore the tools you will find here to help minimize stress and maximize pleasure. Doing so regularly will help you establish a foundation of stability and focus, allowing you to bring your best self forward in every moment.

Do you ever feel like time is spinning faster and faster and it's hard to keep up? Maybe anxious thoughts fill your mind because it seems that there is too much to do and too little time in which to do it, or that you'll never be able to do it all as well as you would like to. Perhaps you are encountering more aches and pains as the years go by. All of these things lead you to breathe faster unconsciously, taking shorter and shallower breaths. The result is that you may live a shorter and shallower life because you are not taking in and absorbing the oxygen you need to thrive.

By developing an awareness of how you breathe and slowing down your breathing, you may become more aware of how you feel, moment by moment, and can use that as a guideline for maintaining and/or improving your physical, mental, and emotional health. Science shows us that when we slow down our breathing, we slow down our lives. (Ref. 1) Our tissues have more time to absorb the nutrients they need to thrive, and we have more time to enjoy all that is unfolding around us. The result is that our ability to respond joyfully to all that life brings our way grows, and we leave our judgmental and reactive nature behind.

As you progress, you will be invited to take slower, deeper breaths and to breathe into your belly. You will also be encouraged to elevate your level of awareness of how you breathe to facilitate a superior sense of ease. Doing these things can help reduce the distress brought about by a busy life.

Consider the word *inspire*. To inspire someone is to stimulate them to think, be, or do something. The word carries with it a sense of impacting, enlivening, and motivating. *Inspire* comes from the Latin, *inspirare*, which combines into (in) with breathe (spirare). The word *spirit* shares the same root, and when we think of spirit as that quality of courage, determination, and soulfulness that humans seek to embody, it is not a stretch to say that there is something courageous, spirited, and inspiring about breathing mindfully. It requires a commitment to bring our awareness to our breath and to do that again and again. But when we do, we have an opportunity to grow more courageous because the act of breathing deepens our connection to the source of strength within us—something we can rely on and tap in to during life's challenging moments. If living well and living courageously calls to you, why not take the time to learn to breathe?

Did you know that humans breathe somewhere around twenty-three thousand times a day? That is almost 8,400,000 breaths a year. As something we do so often, we have plenty of opportunity to refine and improve upon how we breathe. Learning to breathe well will allow you to tap in to the source of who you are and bring that forward into all you do. You will respond more and react less, gaining control over flighty thoughts, feelings, and behaviors.

Try it now. Take in a comfortably long, comfortably slow, deep breath. Sigh it out. Notice how you feel. If that felt good, do it again. While breathing is something each of us does many times every day, how often do you pay attention to how you breathe? My hope is that the material in this book will guide you toward connecting with your breath in a mindful manner to foster greater health on every level of your being: physically, mentally, emotionally, and spiritually.

Holistic health care, a form of alternative or complementary medicine, considers the whole being rather than individual parts when looking at how to minimize dis-ease and elevate well-being. Our breath is what links the various parts of who we are together. Bringing awareness to how you breathe and mindfully fine-tuning your breathing pattern nurtures the sense of feeling more integrated and whole. Courageously breathing with awareness has the potential to enhance your life by minimizing stress and maximizing your ability to focus, achieve, and enjoy life—all at the same time. All you need do is allow yourself to be inspired and step into the little bit of courage it takes to breathe consciously.

Breathing As Healthful Four-Part Harmony

Until we stop to think about it, most of us take breathing for granted. We breathe in and we breathe out. But there are actually two other components to effective breathing: the pause after inhalation (in-breath) and the pause after exhalation (out-breath). Attention can be brought to one part of the breathing process over another at different times to address specific situations, as you will discover, and you will be given practices to help you with that.

Many of the tools you will encounter here have been used for thousands of years to bring about comfort and good health. (Ref 2.) They remain as powerful today as ever, and some of them could even be considered components of a modern-day stress management kit. As a professional yoga therapist and certified holistic stress management educator, I apply several of these practices on a daily basis in my own personal practice, and they leave me feeling more grounded, calm, and confident. I also offer them in my work with clients of all ages and observe similar results. It only takes a few minutes a day to achieve the benefits of a mindful breathing practice.

Consider the process of learning to breathe as a fun adventure. You will be invited to explore and familiarize yourself with the four distinct portions of the breath as you read through the book. If the concept seems foreign, give yourself time to get used to the idea. I invite you to bring a sense of playfulness with you as you engage with the breathing and visualization tools offered here. They will support you in living an inspired life.

Along with the basic breathing practices, I have offered tips on mudra, mantra, counting, and visualization, all of which may serve to deepen your relationship with your breath and elevate your experience of life. Regardless of your age or stage in life, this guide will support you in reclaiming and maintaining a lifelong breathing practice designed to foster your best self.

Those who use the techniques outlined in this book have described increased feelings of well-being. The Belly Breath Practice, which is a way of refining what I call the Easy Breath, is the foundational tool for other techniques in this book. Known to stimulate the restorative aspect of the autonomic nervous system, the parasympathetic nervous system, breathing into the belly instigates the relaxation response in the body. In this way, it helps relieve a variety of stress-related abnormalities including random pain, variations in heart rhythm, digestive issues, and insomnia. (Ref. 3)

In addition, many other conditions stem from unrelinquished demands placed on our time. These demands often lead to the feeling of being stressed, which results in the continued stimulation of the sympathetic nervous system and triggers the fight (anger), flight (fear), or freeze (incapacity) response. What is the result: Low levels of oxygen perfusing the organs and tissues.

If you suffer from fatigue or loss of breath, sleep or memory issues, PTSD, anxiety, depression, blood pressure issues including hypertension, Crohn's disease, or diabetes, what you find in this book may offer relief. While not a substitute for regular medical care, consider the practices in this book to be natural and beneficial complements to traditional health care.

A Peaceful Practice

Each breathing tool may be considered a practice in its own right. But please note that I use several words interchangeably throughout the book, especially the word *practice*. This word is sometimes used to refer to the time we sit each day and explore the tools. Sitting becomes a practice when we return to it again and again. It is not something we need to perfect. Rather, it is something to return to, learning more each time we come back to it. The tools form our practice, and they are what we practice as we sit.

You will find that I refer to the breathing and visualization tools as both techniques and practices. I also refer to breathing with awareness as conscious breathing or mindful breathing. All of these terms get at the same thing: the value of slowing down and paying attention to how we breathe. The bottom line is that the more familiar you become with the techniques, the easier it will be to implement them on an ongoing basis. In doing so, you establish a productive and health-giving practice over time. Becoming more centered and peaceful is a frequent result, and the ability to tap into those feelings in trying times is another.

Medical Disclaimer

While some people have been able to avoid taking medication to address symptoms of pain or other discomfort as a result of improving the way they breathe, and while the practices outlined in this book are beneficial to overall health, they are designed to complement a positive health care regimen, not be a substitute for regular medical care. While they may enhance good feelings in the body and mind over time and may reduce the need for some medications, it is common for some people to feel lightheaded when first initiating conscious breathing exercises. This is because the relationship between carbon dioxide and oxygen levels in the body changes as we take longer, deeper breaths. Your body may need time to adapt to this. Move slowly and know that you will adjust to a more efficient exchange of gases in the body and benefit from greater amounts of oxygen circulating through your tissues. Please talk to your doctor if you have any disturbing symptoms.

Creating A Relaxed And Relaxing Practice

The best way to create a practice and benefit from conscious breathing is to carve out a small amount of time for it every day. It need not take more than five minutes a day to initiate a positive relationship with your breath. Doing this at the same time every day (first thing in the morning upon waking, after showering, once you've sent others off into their day, or in the evening as you prepare for bed) helps establish an effective routine. As you develop familiarity with the practices, you may find you would like to spend more time with them. That's great. Take as much time as you wish and practice breathing as often as you would like, adding to your regular daily sitting time as time and space allow. The benefits will grow as you do this.

Carve out a place to practice as well as a time. It is best to remove yourself from external distractions by finding a private place in which to connect with your breathing in a focused manner. Carving out a place and a time to work with these tools helps you bring them into your daily life. During your practice time, you can sit in a chair, sit on the floor, or lie down. Because many people find that they fall asleep when they lie down to practice, sitting upright is often a good choice.

Sit comfortably with a firm foundation, an erect spine, and relaxed shoulders. Once settled, all you have to do is pay attention to your breath (which may be easier said than done, especially at the start). Notice sensations as breath moves in and out through your nose. Imagine the breath like ocean waves, washing into the shore of the mind and back out again in a soothing and gentle manner. Guide your mind back to the sensations or back to the visualization you are practicing each time it wanders away. In the beginning, your practice may only last for a handful of minutes. That's okay!

Think of a breathing or visualization practice as an opportunity to set aside your to-do list. Take this time out for yourself, to acknowledge and connect with your deepest self, use it as time to listen to your inner voice. This is a chance to offer gentle and loving care to yourself and honor that which you really are, while letting your inner wisdom bubble up and infuse your day. By taking care of yourself in this way, filling yourself up through your practice, you prime yourself to be more available when others really need you.

Familiarize yourself with the Easy Breath first and then add the Belly Breath to that. Through these techniques, you will be invited to explore the four parts of the breath before moving on to additional tools.

As mentioned above, practicing in a relaxed manner will stimulate the parasympathetic nervous system. As this happens and movement is freed in the belly, you may find improvements over time in your digestion, circulation, respiration, elimination, and even sleep. Movement in the belly leads to a heightened sense of relaxation because life force energy, or *prana*, flows more efficiently throughout the entire body.

When you become comfortable with the practices offered in the first part of the book, you will be ready to explore the breath modulations found in later chapters to achieve specific results. Let the experience of release and restoration take hold and call you back to the practice day after day after day.

Bring to your practice a positive attitude and remember to avoid overdoing it. Take your time, allowing your comfort level to grow as you regularly practice for short periods. Regularity will reinforce the irrefutable impact that these practices may have on you. Refine their application along the way if you like. There is no goal or final destination to reach.

As your practice matures, feel free to select individual tools to work with, as needed to address changes in your body, mind, emotions, and environment. The more you apply them, the greater the benefit as time goes on. Not only will you experience immediate changes, you will find that profound and pleasing results will also accrue over time. A sense of repose and centeredness may develop that you can carry over into the rest of your day. My clients have recounted stories of improvements in their health, relationships, and even their finances as effects of using the tools found in this book. Why not feel good as you tackle the challenges of life with increasing levels of confidence, clarity, and joy?

I encourage you to cultivate a sense of curiosity as you work with the tools in this book. Explore the way you feel as you practice. Notice what changes come about afterwards. What are the differences between the various tools, and how do you respond to each of them? Couple your curiosity about what unfolds with the intention that your personal practice serve you in the highest way possible.

Let mindful breathing be your anchor to the here and now, your lifeline when the seas of change are swirling uncontrollably, and you will feel more confident and calm as you navigate life.

1

Breathing In Animates And Oxygenates

Whenever I feel blue, I start breathing again.

-L. Frank Baum

Breath sustains and animates us. Thankfully, breathing is a function in the body that happens whether we think about it or not. Even though it is a part of the autonomic nervous system, which controls the involuntary activities in our bodies, it can be manipulated consciously. Doing so offers a sense of control over how we feel in any given moment.

Breathe in and notice how you feel. It may be that right now, you feel no different than you did before. But you are not only bringing air into the lungs when you inhale, you are also facilitating a gaseous exchange, which helps cleanse and fuel every cell in your body. With practice, bringing more awareness to *how* you breathe may change the *way* you breathe to change the way you feel, in part because of the influence of body chemistry. Focusing your awareness on how you breathe is the first step in facilitating a positive change in your health and overall well-being. Allow your awareness to guide you.

Connecting With Life Force Energy

Long ago in India, people realized that the way we breathe could be manipulated in specific ways to facilitate various outcomes. This understanding came about by tuning in to the subtle quality of the breath, which is an energy that permeates the entire body. They called this energy prana. The practice of breathing intentionally and with awareness is called pranayama, and it is a common application in the field of yoga.

The word *pranayama* is an ancient Sanskrit term that refers to the way one might manipulate the breath to achieve specific results. It also refers to the science of breathing. The first part of the word, *prana*, refers to life force energy, which travels on the breath. This is the same energy that is called *chi* in traditional Chinese medicine and *ki* in Japanese medicine. Mystical Christian traditions allude to it as the *Holy Ghost*, also considered the *Great Spirit* by some Native Americans.

While the lungs fill with breath, prana, or life force energy, travels through the entire body, nourishing us at the cellular level. Fine-tuning your awareness of the breath leads to a heightened awareness of energy flow. As your practice grows more refined, you may notice how prana permeates your entire body each time you breathe in. As you become adept at this, you can consider whether to restrain a component of the breath or breathe without restraint to facilitate specific results.

In Sanskrit, the second part of the word *pranayama* may be broken out as *yama*, often translated as restraint or *ayama*, which means without restraint. Both apply to the manner in which we take breath in, hold it, and release it out from the body. Understanding the translation of this ancient word may assist you in becoming conscious of the subtle effects that breathing can have on your body, mind, emotions, and spirit. Breathing can be manipulated to increase energy, decrease intense reactions to acute situations, or simply to nourish your body and mind. With time, you may become skilled at modifying your breath to feel more alert, vibrant, and content.

You can also use breath to unite all parts of who you are and to link yourself to everything around you. Taking a conscious breath in is the first step in learning to breathe.

Playing With Pranayama

In yoga, pranayama practices are used as tools for deepening one's connection to the flow of life force energy. There is an energetic pathway which is referred to in ancient texts as the divine body and often called the subtle body through which this energy travels. As air fills our lungs, prana moves through this energetic pathway, nourishing us on many levels. It also helps to calm the mind by providing an inner focus for our attention. These actions are what transform breathing, which is often an unconscious act, into art.

Art, like play, integrates the two hemispheres of the brain, allowing us to bring our whole selves into what we're doing. When you explore breathing practices (pranayama) in a playful manner, consider the artful actions that have the power to transform the stresses of modern living. The result may be that your whole world appears brighter and more buoyant.

Beginning now, you are invited to consider how you breathe. Establish an awareness of how you breathe, and seek to do so in a light and playful manner. As you progress, you may naturally begin to take longer, slower, more comfortable breaths. Continue this to initiate a positive lifelong relationship with your breath, and it will support you in bringing your whole self into all you *do* and support you in *being* all you are meant to be.

Just Breathe…

Find Your Own Way To Be

The art of breathing is really about *being*, rather than *doing*. While the act of breathing is natural to all of us, each person's pranayama practice will be unique. Let yours develop over time. Some find that they really like the nourishing quality that comes when they take time to breathe in more deeply than they have been used to doing. Some enjoy a sense of deep rest available to them during the pauses between the in-breath (inhalation) and out-breath (exhalation). Others find that they prefer to focus on the exhalation because it facilitates the release of stress and strain, and in so doing, it helps them maintain a balanced level of energy throughout challenging experiences. Regardless of what your experience is, remaining mindful of how you breathe often brings improvements that are pleasant and compelling over time.

Ancient Wisdom

Wisdom from age-old traditions tells us that a longer, fuller breath leads to a longer, fuller life. These traditions tell us that the life span of a person is measured by the number of breaths they take. Swara yogis, those who concern themselves with the science of yogic breathing, believe that if a person breathes at an average rate of fifteen breaths per minute (which means that each breath lasts approximately four seconds) throughout their lifetime, they may very well live for 120 years. Modern science is starting to prove what the ancients experienced long ago, which is that the energy, or prana, that travels on the breath is what brings life to the whole body and that when we slow down our breathing rate, our bodies more deeply absorb prana. (Ref. 4)

Conscious breathing, qigong, yoga, acupuncture, and reiki are techniques with historic roots that work with this energy flow by manipulating the channels in the subtle body through which life force energy flows. Traditionally, these techniques have been used to slow us down so that we might focus on the integration between the body, mind (as both intellect and emotion), and soul. The result is that we move away from stress and move toward a more intimate relationship with the essence of who we are. In this way, we more effectively connect with the flow of life within us and all around us.

Benefits Of A Pranayama Practice

- Calms the mind, increasing ability to focus
- Stabilizes the emotions, minimizing mood swings
- Nourishes the body down to the cellular level
- Familiarizes us with the many aspects of who we are
- Facilitates bringing out our best selves in all we do

Breathe In Again and Notice: Refining Awareness

This is a good time to bring your awareness to your breath again. Take a full breath in now. Pay attention to how you feel as you do this. Notice what parts of your body move as you breathe in. Can you ascribe qualities to the way you breathe? Was the breath you just took a short breath or a long one, a deep breath or a shallow breath? Was breathing in easy or challenging? Did you notice any restriction in your breathing? Become curious and mindful of your breathing.

Deepening your awareness of how you breathe can lead to positive changes in how you feel. Let's take it one step—one breath—at a time.

2

Cultivating The Art Of An Easy Breath

The pursuit, even of the best things, ought to be calm and tranquil.

-Marcus Tullius Cicero

What is an easy breath you ask? It is the first step on the journey toward establishing, maintaining, or reclaiming radiant good health. It may reflect a refinement of the way you breathe. An easy breath is one that is conscious, fluid, and smooth, and it lends a sense of calmness and security to body and mind. Associated with an easy breath is the ability to breathe on a horizontal plane rather than up and down. By this, I mean that when you take an easy breath, your tummy and ribs, your torso, and even your chest seem to expand *out* as you breathe in. There is no lifting of the shoulders. Like the slow and rhythmic movement of placid ocean waves washing elegantly onto the shore and then merging again with their source, the ocean, your breath expands you into your fullness while connecting you with the source of your being. Allow it to move effortlessly and expand in all directions as you take it in and release it out.

As a foundation for the other practices presented in this book, crafting an easy breath will set you up to fully benefit from additional breathing tools. The first step in this is to tell yourself that the time you devote to cultivating an awareness of how you breathe is time well spent. Doing this not only leads to a calmer mind, it also nourishes the tissues of your body in a health giving way.

Paying Attention

Please find a secluded spot where you will be left alone for a period of time. Once settled, take note of how you feel in both body and mind. Can you describe how you feel *right now*? Do you feel in a hurry to move through this book so you can minimize stress right away? Are you anxious or are you doubting the effectiveness of these practices? Perhaps you are curious about the tools and eager to learn. Are you aware of any tension in your body? Maybe you feel tired after a long and demanding day or a restless night of sleep. It may be unfamiliar to probe your experience in this way, but doing so is the way to effect positive change. As you ponder thoughts, feelings, and sensations, breathe as you are used to. Breathe in a way that is natural and normal for you.

It's natural to feel uncertain about change and want to avoid it, wondering about what might unfold as you engage with conscious breathing. Common responses to change include fear, anxiety, passivity, and doubt. Your mind (which some would refer to as the ego here) may be thinking that things are moving way too slowly right now and telling you that you have better things to do with your time. Or it may be worrying about how much work this is going to be, or what might happen when you change the way you breathe. That's okay. While we are not always aware of the workings of our mind, wondering about these things is normal. Often, our fears and concerns impact us less when we acknowledge them, and we learn to courageously move ahead in spite of them. What's important is to move forward slowly so the nervous system has time to unwind as you progress. That will lead to success.

As your ability to observe experiences in your body and your mind grows stronger, the flow of your breath will grow stronger too. Soon, you may find that you become less distracted by activities outside of you and are better able to focus on the task at hand, be it breathing mindfully, balancing your bank account, preparing for an exam, or making decisions pertinent to the success of your company. With time, you may be able to maintain awareness of your breath flow without being pulled off center by thoughts, which is quite a pleasant experience.

As you learn to relax into the experience of breathing, little exertion is needed. You allow the breath to move with minimal effort, releasing the need to manage or control it. As a result, you may become more aware of the sources of stress in your life and be able to address them effectively if that is your desire.

Then you are in the driver's seat for managing your health. It all begins by artfully cultivating an easy breath.

Cultivating The Art Of An Easy Breath, Part One

- In a distraction free environment, sit or lie down. Take awareness out of your head and place it in your body. Sink your awareness down into the support of the chair, couch, bed, or floor beneath you.
- Now, breathe in deeply and sigh out your breath. Breathe that way again, two or three times. If you are able to, breathe in through your nose and release the breath with an obvious and perhaps loud sigh through the mouth. Sighing helps release tension and brings us into the present moment.
- Then rest for a moment. Breathe naturally. Pay attention to how you feel. What do you notice? Your breath rate may have slowed. Tension may have diminished. Can you tell if you feel any different than before you took those deep breaths?

Refining your ability to note how you feel moment-by-moment may become a pleasant side effect of heightened breath awareness. As mentioned before, this is what turns the act of breathing into an art. Establish that super power and you're on your way to cultivating the art of an easy breath.

Cultivating The Art Of An Easy Breath, Part Two

When you are ready for more, again focus your awareness on the movement of breath into and out from your body. If possible, breathe in and out only through your nose now and smooth out your breath as you go. Imagine a central channel or energetic column running up and down through your body, connecting the crown of your head with your tailbone. As you breathe in, invite your whole torso to expand out in all directions from that central column. Allow it to recede back in as you exhale. Take three to five rounds of breath in this way. Then pause and breathe as you typically do when not giving it much thought.

Find Your Calm By Taking Deeper And Slower Breaths

Stress management gurus tell us that unconscious breath restraint—as in the case of a busy, frightened, or harried person who breathes shallowly—causes stress levels to elevate. Some people experience headaches, fatigue, anxiety, or depression as a result. Taking quick, short, shallow breaths is inefficient because air often reaches only the upper lobes of the lungs. This causes us to breathe faster to collect the oxygen that our tissues need to function. As our breathing rate increases, body tissues have little time to absorb the oxygen they need. The sympathetic or excitatory nervous system is stimulated and cortisol levels increase, resulting in a cascade of negative impacts. Over time, we may grow tired, lethargic, and perhaps even ill.

In contrast, taking slower, deeper, and more complete breaths helps us feel more vital and relaxed. In part, this happens because air is traveling deeper into the lungs and more oxygen is available for use by the body's cells. Deep and easy breathing has a positive effect on the nervous system. It allays the fight, flight, or freeze response of the sympathetic nervous system that is exacerbated by modern daily living.

With greater amounts of oxygen coming in to the body due to deeper, slower breathing, the nervous system—brain included—has a chance to rest, and hormone levels even out. Balance, or homeostasis, then returns to all body systems. As this happens, health improves. Cultivating an easy breath is a great first step in this process.

Rooting Into Awareness

It is common for the obligations and activities of daily living to pull awareness up into the mind and out into the world around you. When that happens, you become less aware of what's going on inside yourself. Making time in your day to sit and concentrate on how you breathe pulls awareness back into your body.

Try this now: Whether you are standing or sitting, imagine that you can anchor down into the energy of the earth. Sink your awareness into your feet. Allow your bottom half to root while your spine rises up out of the pelvis. Apply as little effort as possible while doing this.

Now, imagine a tall tree sinking roots deep into the earth. The roots nourish and energize the tree. The branches and leaves reach for the sunlight in the sky. Become like a tree. Does that contribute to feeling more grounded and stable?

As you establish this in your body, your mind may find repose as well. Over time, this grounding exercise supports the establishment of a long, languid, resting breath. In that way, breath becomes nourishing, and you mindfully connect with the steady pulsation of life force energy that enters your body with it. Connecting with life force energy can reveal your essential nature, which is centered and whole. By rooting into awareness and cultivating a beneficial resting breath, you may catch a glimpse of who you really are.

Root to Rise and Thrive

3

Opening To The Mystery

All things share the same breath—the beast, the tree, the man. The air shares its spirit with all the life it supports.

-Chief Seattle

When I think about breathing, I find it to be a mysterious and interesting act. Like ocean waves, it is a rhythmic force, one that ebbs and flows, continuing whether we think about it or not. And it connects us to everything around us. I like how we can modify and control this bodily function in beneficial ways. Imagine what it might be like to breathe without any restraint placed on your breathing. Imagine your breath flowing fluidly, as naturally as it did when you were a baby. Open to the mystery of breathing by cultivating awareness of it. Allow it to move through you in a smooth and effortless manner, much like those gentle ocean waves that wash onto the shore and then recede back into their source with admirable ease.

Breathe consciously again now. Notice its qualities, as you have done before. Is your breath typically smooth, easy, and deep, or is it quick and short? When you are stressed, it is natural to tense up and breathe shallowly. As your awareness increases, you may want to manipulate such things as the pace and depth of the breath, exploring the consequences of this. Let your intention be to establish a breath that is less restricted, more natural and effortless.

Many practitioners refer to the two obvious parts of the breath—inhalation and exhalation—when considering breath work. I guide a four-part breath that highlights the pauses in between these two basic components of breathing because they offer critical moments for transformation. As a mirror of the four parts of a human being (body, mind, emotion, and spirit) that contribute to our wholeness, each part of a four-part breath—the in-breath, the out-breath, and the pauses in between—can be refined as you develop your breathing practice.

Please note that if you suffer from chronic illness, it is best to maintain a smooth and easy breath flow that is not restricted in any way. Consider the pauses to be the place where the breath flow *turns around.* What I mean by that is that you may experience a short pause as an inhalation comes to an end and changes to an exhalation. That may also occur after your breath has emptied out and before it travels in again. These are the pauses I am referring to, though there is no active holding of the breath.

Consider each of these four parts now. Breathe all the way in. Pause. Breathe all the way out. Pause. What do you observe? Clients tell me that when they pay attention to the four parts of the breath, which really means paying attention to the pauses in the breath cycle, they feel calmer. Some describe a circular quality to the flow of their breath. They share how the pace of life seems to slow down when they breathe consciously, and they become more engaged with their lives.

Modifications to the way we breathe have been explored for thousands of years to bring about comfort and good health. At their foundation is the Easy Breath Practice, which you have done. As you may have already discerned, the easy breath is a comfortably full, comfortably slow and flowing breath that moves like soft ocean waves. It is a natural breath that moves in and out in a languid manner and has natural, comfortable pauses woven into it.

Four Parts To A Breath, Four Chances To Unwind

Let's further explore the four parts of the breath using an easy breath as the foundation. Here's how:

- ➢ The inhalation is the first part of a four-part breath. The act of inhaling supports you in living a good life. Inhaling brings oxygen and vital energy into the lungs, perfusing the entire body. Without an adequate inhalation, your tissues begin to die.
- ➢ Pausing after you inhale, if only briefly, provides space and time for vital energy (prana), which enters the body as you inhale, to circulate throughout the body. This pause offers a moment to consider breathing refinements that might serve you best in the moment.

- When exhaling, you are invited to release effort and stress. Consider the exhalation as a release valve. It provides an opportunity to let go of tension and strain. It is also a chance to release any expectation of results in your breathing practice. There will be times when you will choose to lengthen this component of the breath cycle because doing so provides release.
- The final piece in a four-part breath is the pause following the exhalation. It provides a space in which you may find yourself unexpectedly, effortlessly, and beautifully merging with the world around you, or possibly transcending the physical world. Just as rest complements action, pausing is an important component of the breath cycle. This pause enhances your ability to absorb and enjoy the fruits that come from conscious breathing before repeating the four-part breathing cycle again.

As you engage with the four-part breath over time, you may find that the experience not only melts away stress but also enhances alertness and improves overall health.

The Benefits Of Nose Breathing

Did you know that nose breathing, as opposed to mouth breathing, further stimulates the relaxation response in the body? Nose breathing is an important component of the Easy Breath Practice. Science tells us that breathing in and out through the nose, and breathing into the belly, stimulates the parasympathetic nervous system (PNS). This, in turn, causes us to relax. The PNS facilitates rest and digestion, functions that work most efficiently when we feel safe and calm and alleviate stress. (Ref. 5)

By contrast, the short, shallow breaths that constitute both mouth and chest breathing stimulate the sympathetic nervous system (SNS) and cause our brain to believe that danger exists all around us. When we continuously live in this aroused state, we grow anxious, irritable, and depressed. We may have trouble with digestion and the quality of our sleep is affected. In short, we experience less joy in life. Learning to breathe well through the nose is the antidote to this.

Again, I invite you to explore how you feel by taking a few more rounds of easy breath. Noticing changes may take time, and modifying the way you breathe can take some getting used to, especially if your preferred way of breathing is through the mouth. For many, a pronounced sense of serenity comes to the body and mind after taking three or four conscious, deep breaths through the nose.

Others become lightheaded when they breathe in this way for an extended time, mainly because it is not something they are used to doing. We become lightheaded because the gas exchange in the body is changing. When one is not used to breathing as we've been practicing, a period of adjustment to the more efficient uptake of oxygen is needed. Before advancing, it is important to note that if you ever feel lightheaded or dizzy, stop breathing in any prescribed way and rest for a few moments. Go back to breathing as is customary for you until these feelings subside. They should lessen as you move forward.

Another reason to breathe through the nose is that there are filters in the nose that help remove irritants and pollutants from the air you breathe. As the air travels through the nose, it is warmed and moisturized. The mouth takes a portion of the air meant for the lungs into the stomach. This leads to belching and for some, anxiety.

Benefits Of Nose Breathing

- Warms, moisturizes, and filters the air coming in
- Takes air deeper into the lungs than mouth breathing
- Stimulates the body's relaxation response
- Facilitates better transport of waste products out of the body
- Exercises the diaphragm, allowing for more complete breaths
- Massages the stomach, heart, and lungs, leading to improved digestion and circulation
- Increases alpha brain wave activity, which fosters a meditative state

Modify the way you breathe as needed to accompany your particular situation. What's important is to deepen and slow down the rate at which you breathe and, when you have practiced enough to do so, take more breaths in through your nose than through your mouth. Remember to use as little effort as possible. If you are new to breath awareness activities or feel lightheaded after you attempt this technique, practice for shorter amounts of time and include more practice sessions throughout the course of the day. As implementing the Easy Breath Practice becomes comfortable, you will realize that it doesn't take much time and that when you come back to it for short periods of time throughout the day, it serves as an antidote to the stresses of a busy life. The easy breath, which is a way to describe aware and restful breathing through the nose, may soon become your preferred way of breathing.

Minding What Matters Brings Focus To An Active Mind

As you become mindful of breathing, you may begin to notice how full and busy your mind is. You may also notice how that busyness can distract you from focusing on breathing, and cause you to be more reactive to disturbances of your time and space. Becoming mindful of your breath may lead to quieter actions in the body, and the mind may follow suit. At the same time, the activity level of the mind becomes more noticeable. Perhaps you have experienced this when you've crawled into bed at night? The mind stresses over the activities of the day or races forward to what you have planned for the next day, instead of dropping into a quiet state, even though the body may be worn out and ready to rest. Taking a few minutes to breathe mindfully as you transition from your day may relieve this. With practice, over time, the act of breathing will soften into an effortless art and the mind activity may settle down a bit.

To counter a busy mind, it's helpful to pay attention to your thoughts instead of trying to push them away. See if you can catch your thoughts as they enter your mind. A great mind management technique is to label each thought as *thinking* as soon as you notice it, and then do your best to let the thought float away. This is much like noticing large, fluffy clouds as they pass across a blue sky on a warm summer day. This helps withdraw awareness from the mind and place it back on your breath. Let thoughts float across the sky of the mind, noticing them without becoming attached to them, as you direct awareness back to observing the flow of breath in and out through the nose.

If you do this with loving attention over time, thoughts, mind, and breath begin to merge harmoniously together during our practice. This is a wonderfully relaxing state, and the result may lead to an elevated level of focus in your practice and in your life.

Give The Mind A Job

Another way to work with a busy mind is to give it a job. When your mind is racing or scattered, ask it to take charge of watching the breathing process. This opens you to the mystery of the breath and allows the breath to act as a focal point for the mind. As a result, the mind often grows calmer.

At first, the mind might seem like a small child, needing to be guided back to the task and gently reminded to remain focused. Yet this is an important task that you are assigning to the mind. In time, the mind may acquiesce and engage with the breathing activities more easily instead of wandering into memories from the past or plans for the future. Notice how you feel then. When this happens, you have an ally in the process of conscious breathing. That is an appropriate time to further refine your breathing practice.

Yet another technique for focusing the mind is to pay attention to sensation. With the mind's help, see if you can discern the sensations that occur as the breath enters and exits the nostrils. Do sensations differ between the in-breath and the out-breath or from one nostril to the other? What is happening in the body as you inhale? What happens during the pauses? Do you feel differently once you've exhaled all your breath out compared to after you took it in? This exercise builds mental acuity.

Use the mind in this way and stimulate curiosity about the act of breathing. Ask your mind to note where life force energy travels as breath fills and empties your lungs. Heightened awareness of what is happening all over your body is often a result of this practice. For those who have experienced a traumatic situation that caused awareness to travel out of the body, this curiosity may lead you back in to it in a safe and gentle manner. It may lead you to a place of superior relaxation and elevate your ability to focus and to trust in the process of life as it unfolds both around you and deep within you.

An Invitation To Pause

The ability to become mindful of your breath, and move awareness into your body as you grow more comfortable inhaling longer, deeper breaths comes by befriending the Easy Breath Practice. Now is the time to build on that. Pause before proceeding to acknowledge your progress, to note effects, and to ask your whole self if you are ready to deepen your pranayama practice.

By this point, I hope you have become comfortable taking more breath in and are able to focus on breathing for longer periods of time each day. Refining your awareness may lead you to notice the natural tendency to pause ever so slightly after the inhalation has ended, before you exhale. It's as if the breath is taking a moment to change directions from moving in to moving out. Connect with this pause and you will deepen your relationship with the breath. It is the pauses between the cycles of breath that lead us from what is becoming a nourishing breath to experiencing what can become transformational well-being. Why not let mindful breathing transform the way you live?

4

BEFRIENDING THE BELLY BREATH

The pearl is in the oyster.

The oyster is in the bottom of the ocean. Dive deep.

-Ancient Sufi Poet, Kabir

Belly Breathing Practice is a wonderful tool for alleviating stress and invigorating your life because it naturally triggers the relaxation response in our bodies. While it is true that you are only breathing into your lungs, for this exercise, imagine that you could breathe all the way down into your belly. I want you to imagine that your lungs can extend into your abdomen as they fill with air. Urge your breath to expand in all directions each time you inhale. As you exhale, let the belly contract as breath empties out from your lungs.

When you let the belly expand as you inhale, the diaphragm, a large muscle that separates the chest cavity from the abdominal cavity, drops toward the belly. Not only does this give the organs in the belly a tender massage, it makes room for more breath to enter the lungs. During the exhalation, the act of contracting the belly sends the diaphragm up toward the chest again, pressing air from the lungs.

These actions in the belly also stimulate the vagus nerve, a key player in the parasympathetic nervous system (PNS), promoting the ability to rest. What's more, we can take bigger breaths because the diaphragm—the largest muscle of respiration that lies all the way across the torso near the base of the lungs and separates the chest cavity from the abdominal cavity—moves out of the way. These conditions allow you to grow more sensitive to actions in your belly, including your innate "gut instincts". You gain a stronger connection to the powerful resource of intuition, which allows for more holistic decision-making than just relying on the mind.

Let's Belly Breathe

Return to a place where you will be uninterrupted and peaceful for an extended period of time. Settle into a steady and rooted position with an upright spine and relaxed shoulders and body.

- Initiate an easy breath, expanding out in all directions as you breathe in, and releasing this when you breathe out.
- As your mind and body relax, sink your awareness into your belly. Notice whether it moves as you breathe.
- As you breathe, keep your awareness centered in the abdominal region. Physically expand your belly as you inhale. Contract it as you exhale. Do this several times before resting for a few moments to breathe naturally.
- When engaging in the Belly Breathing Practice, use the pause following each inhalation to consider the residual effects of breathing this way. Use the pause following the exhalation to rest and potentially merge with the source of your breath.
- Remember that when you mindfully expand your belly as you inhale, you allow the diaphragm to drop and the lungs to open to greater volumes of air. Pause to

absorb a greater intake of both oxygen and prana before exhaling.

- When you consciously initiate the contraction on the exhalation, it helps release greater amounts of air out from the lungs. Invite your belly to draw in as you breathe out. Pause again after the exhalation and rest in the blissful state of non-doing.
- Repeat the above actions three to five times in a row, adding repetitions as the practice grows comfortable.

Remember to breathe slowly and easily, without rushing. Rest when tired. There is no point in working to exhaustion because doing so will only impede your progress. Invite the qualities of ease and joy into your experience to support relaxation. With alert and effortless effort, allow the Belly Breathing Practice to take form, breathing while stimulating movement in your belly for several rounds and extending the number of rounds you practice as you grow comfortable with these movements.

Uncertainty And Tension In The Belly

Are you feeling uncertain about the Belly Breathing Practice or are you struggling to move the belly as prescribed? You may place your hands on your belly as you breathe to heighten awareness. Rest your palms on the lowest part of your belly, below your navel, and permit movement to travel all the way down there. Imagine your lungs expanding into your belly and into your hands as you breathe in. Ask your abdomen to stretch and expand into your hands as you inhale and let it fall away each time you exhale.

For a variety of reasons, many of us have developed tension in the belly. Some of us have been taught to keep a tight belly for aesthetic or athletic reasons. For others, the tension has accrued over time as they have been affected by negative and stressful circumstances. Regardless of its source, holding tension in the belly brings about tension in our lives. Drawing awareness into the belly and granting it permission to expand and contract as we breathe helps release tension (in both body and mind) that we no longer need.

Some people have taken on patterns of reverse breathing, recognized by the shoulders rising and the belly tightening as one inhales and a collapse through the solar plexus on the exhalation. They find Belly Breathing Practice quite foreign, and establishing this valuable practice may take time for them. If you are among these people, know that taking the time to befriend belly breathing is worth it because it will lead to greater ease in both body and mind.

Because the lungs are organs, rather than muscles, they don't move on their own. They rely on the diaphragm and several other important muscles to move them. The muscles of respiration—particularly the diaphragm—facilitate the act of breathing. The diaphragm moves when the belly moves, which is why learning to do this is paramount in learning how to breathe. The lungs fill and empty in a most efficient manner when we engage in Belly Breathing Practice.

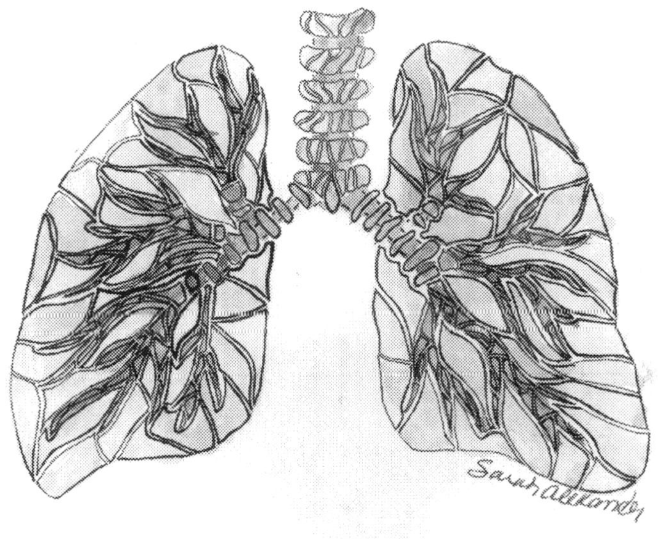

The Lungs Are Organs

Belly Breathing On The Back Minimizes Struggle

If you're having trouble, don't give up. Try belly breathing by lying down on your back. The firmness of the floor, or even a couch or bed, will offer potent feedback about how well you are expanding into the abdominal region. It is a great way to explore the idea of expanding *out*. As suggested above, place your hands on your lower belly once you are comfortably reclining. Inhale and imagine your whole torso expanding.

Your back may press into the floor. Your belly should rise up under your hands. As you exhale, it should feel as if your back, belly, and chest are compressing inward. Do this a number of times, patiently exploring the gentle expansion and contraction of the belly with each breath before pausing to rest.

You may continue to practice belly breathing on your back until it becomes easy and natural. That is the time to progress to a seated posture. Once belly breathing seems natural in the seated position, try it while standing.

This form of breathing may eventually become your go-to style in any situation where you desire a calm, centered, and pleasant demeanor.

Key Points To Consider

- Engage in Belly Breathing Practice for brief periods of time on a regular basis, seeking to establish an effortless effort. Focusing on it for a longer period of time less often will not get you the results that dedicated daily action will.

- Bring loving attention to your body and let this influence your day-to-day practice, trusting that this way of breathing will soon get easier and seem more natural.
- Take your time. Belly Breathing Practice is not only foundational to the remaining tools in this book, it is an important stress mitigation tool in its own right.

The Science Of Belly Breathing

Belly breathing is also called diaphragmatic breathing because the movement of the diaphragm is an important component of this kind of breathing. Both ancient wisdom and modern science tell us that when we breathe into our bellies, we stimulate the relaxation response. (Ref. 6/7) The tremendous thing is that we may thoughtfully choose to do this. As discussed in the bullet points above, use the pause between breaths to soften the belly just before inhaling, giving the diaphragm permission to drop into the abdomen. This, in part, is what causes the lateral expansion of the belly when we breathe in.

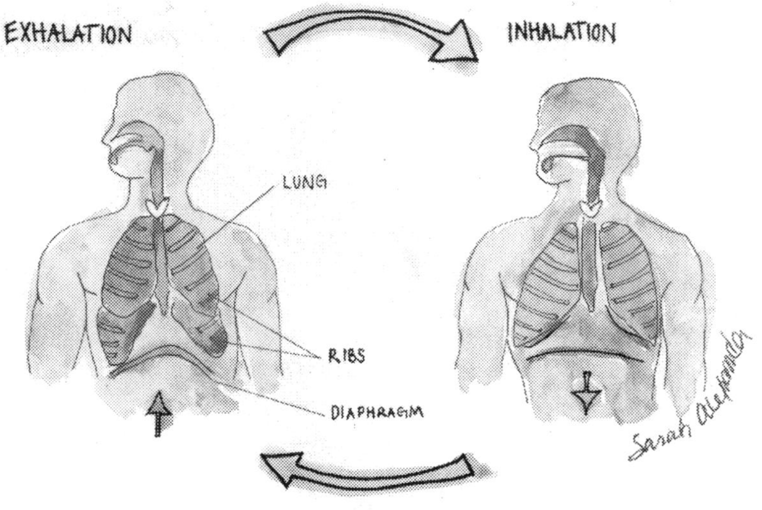

Inhale, expand. Exhale, release.

As the diaphragm moves downwards, the air pressure in the chest cavity changes. This draws air into the lungs. Near the end of the inhalation, the diaphragm moves up toward the chest again. The belly contracts, and this initiates a release of air from the lungs. If you ever have the chance to watch a healthy baby breathe, please do. Babies are not yet bipedal, they have not yet become self-conscious, and they have not yet developed all of their muscles. This allows their bellies to move in an unrestricted manner as they breathe. Babies are natural belly breathers. We all once breathed just like that.

Often, it is only when we feel safe that our belly moves. This guides our body's systems into an efficient rest and digest mode, as mentioned before. In this state of relaxation, tension decreases and greater levels of blood move in from the periphery of the body to nourish the organs in our belly and chest. As our breath deepens and brings movement into the belly, the body systems function in a smooth and more efficient manner. In short, consciously moving your belly with each breath reduces stress, in part because of the way it leads the body/mind toward feeling safe and nourishes our deeper parts. Implement belly breathing, and feel the difference.

Anxiously Waiting For Safety

Stress causes us to unconsciously contract the diaphragm, resulting in shorter, shallower breaths. This happens because the brain perceives a threat and tells the body to shore up resources in the event that you may need to fight, flee, or freeze to remain safe. The body shunts blood away from inner organs and out to the periphery, fueling the large muscles of the legs and arms that may be needed in an escape or a fight. This is a physiological response that we inherited. It harkens back to the day when we were hunting and gathering much of our food and had to worry about becoming a meal instead of finding one.

Nowadays, things have changed. Many of us are no longer concerned only with providing food, nor do we take the time to rest when our bellies are full. Modern urban living brings stressors of a different kind, many of which never subside. It is more difficult for the brain to discern the action needed when it is under a constant barrage of stimulation from cell phones, traffic noises, and unrelenting schedules.

If you are among those navigating through these kinds of stresses, then what happens over time is that the functioning of your diaphragm and all of your bodily systems is diminished, leading to trouble. Learning to sit quietly and breathe into the belly is a terrific antidote to the ceaseless activity in and around you. The quality of your breathing signals to your body that it is either safe or unsafe to rest. Under stress, the muscles of respiration can become unbalanced and a pattern of short, shallow breathing, which lends itself to feelings of anxiousness and unrest, becomes the norm. Mindful awareness of both your body and the quality of your breathing in any given moment is a wonderful first step in quelling stress, and Belly Breathing Practice is one of the keys to inviting in a sense of safety and relaxation.

Diaphragmatic Breathing And The Autonomic Nervous System

Knowing how the nervous system works will help bring all of this into focus. The nervous system has two main components: the central nervous system and the peripheral nervous system. These two components work together to control all of our thoughts and movements, whether they are voluntary or involuntary. The central nervous system is comprised of the brain and the spinal cord. The peripheral nervous system consists of nerve bundles that link the outlying parts of the body to the central nervous system. The autonomic nervous system is a part of the peripheral nervous system, along with the somatic nervous system. The autonomic nervous system acts unconsciously for the most part, regulating heart rate, circulation, respiratory rate, pupillary response, digestion, excretion, sexual arousal, and other bodily functions. The somatic nervous system governs our body's voluntary actions and reflexes.

Within the autonomic nervous system fall the sympathetic nervous system and the parasympathetic nervous system, which are key players in our stress response. As discussed earlier, the sympathetic nervous system activates the fight, flight, or freeze response to stress in our bodies while the parasympathetic nervous system facilitates relaxation, or what some refer to as the rest and digest or feed and breed response.

Through these opposing actions, these two complimentary systems of the autonomic nervous system work moment by moment to facilitate homeostasis or harmony and balance within all of the body's systems. By honing your awareness of the impacts of stress and fine-tuning your ability to belly breathe through stressful experiences, you positively influence system-wide health.

The Role Of The Wandering Vagus Nerve And The Benefit Of Rest

An important player in the peripheral nervous system is the vagus nerve. Researchers primarily associate this nerve—which wanders from the brain through the throat and chest and into the belly—with actions of a restful nature. By communicating with the brain about the state of the organs in your chest and belly, this nerve supports the body in establishing balance. After exertion, it guides the body toward rest. In an ideal world, we have time to rest, and that serves to balance exertion, which maintains homeostasis. The problem comes when our lives are full of more stimulation, busyness, and stress than rest, pleasure, and beneficial recreation.

When stressed, the sympathetic nervous system responds to what it perceives as an impending fight, flight, or freeze situation by releasing stress hormones, including the neurotransmitters cortisol and adrenaline. When released into the body, these hormones support the actions needed to escape from a potential threat. Circulation is shunted from the core of the body to the periphery, allowing us to run faster. Breathing becomes shallow and breath rate increases to fuel the actions needed for escape.

In a perfect world, once all signs of danger have vanished, the vagus nerve (which some refer to as the love nerve) stimulates the release of acetylcholine, a calming neurotransmitter. This mitigates the stress response. As long as we feel safe, our bodies can rest again. Digestion begins. Tense muscles release and are refueled.

Consider this example. When a rabbit runs in front of your car and barely escapes with its life, the release of cortisol and adrenaline allows it to continue running until it finds a safe place to hide and rest. Once safe, the animal rests until its body has recovered from the stressor. Rest and recovery take place because the stress hormones stop secreting and the relaxation hormones take over for the time being. Once recovered, the rabbit is able to go about its normal functions of eating, reproducing, and sleeping. This continues until the next stressor emerges and this natural cycle repeats itself.

Calming neurotransmitters are what the vagus nerve secretes in its communication role in the body. Via numerous branches and tendrils that extend into the organs along its path, this wandering nerve releases enzymes and proteins in addition to acetylcholine such as prolactin, vasopressin, and oxytocin, all of which serve to calm us. When these delightfully relaxing hormones are secreted, we feel less stressed. Once calm, we may even move toward feeling peaceful and content. Life is good.

In such a state, it's both easier and more natural to take breaths that are comfortably long, comfortably slow, and nourishing. When the nervous system relaxes, the breath also drops deeper into the belly. In this way, we move out of the unconscious and very stressful fight or flight mode. What results is a greater ability to rest and to digest not just food, but all of life's experiences. That is the hallmark of the parasympathetic nervous system.

Why Learn The Art Of Belly Breathing?

Is the wisdom behind the Belly Breathing Practice now making sense? When the belly expands, we are able to take deeper, more efficient breaths. These powerful breaths calm the body, focus the mind, and lead us out of stress mode. With practice, I think you will find that belly breathing leaves you feeling present, positive, peppy, and pleased as you move through each day, regardless of the amount of stress in your life. Regular practice of this profound pranayama technique may even help you sleep better at night.

As this method of breathing becomes comfortable and familiar, try applying it in other places and at other times of day, in addition to continuing your regularly scheduled daily practice.

What's nice is that belly breathing can be used as a stand-alone practice anytime and anywhere to soothe your body, focus your mind, enhance digestion, or help you remember what's important. Apply it in your car when you are stopped at a traffic light or when you are standing in a long line at the grocery store. It's also a great tool to use in the waiting room at the doctor's or dentist's office. What's fun is that no one else needs to know what you are doing. You may soon find that it becomes your go-to practice in many stressful situations.

Allow Instead Of Force

Rather than striving to "get it," simply allow the process to unfold organically. The muscles of respiration are growing stronger and more united with each application of belly breathing. Keep bringing your awareness back to the belly each time you inhale because that is what fosters proficient breaths and advantageous relaxation over time. The amount of time it takes to befriend the belly breath varies from one person to the next. Allow that to unfold, too. There is no need to rush through this tool to get to the next one.

Important Belly Breathing Points

- Make sure that your Belly Breathing Practice is well established before moving on. It is foundational to an exceptional practice.
- Breathe comfortably deep and expand the abdominal area in all directions on inhalation. Let it contract each time you exhale. Keep the shoulders quiet and relaxed, dropping away from your ears.
- Notice how you feel. Did you feel this way when you first opened this book? Celebrate successes along the way!
- Assign the mind the important task of focusing on sensation and following body and belly movements as you breathe. This way, you train your mind to let go of thoughts and rest in a more peaceful state.

Refining Your Awareness

For those exploring further, I want to point out that over time, as your awareness increases and your breath grows deeper, you may begin to notice that after you breathe into the belly, the expansion created on the inhale starts there, and then moves up the back, opening the ribcage and even the chest area more. This is subtle and beneficial. It is the result of taking what yogis call a full body breath. While this is an advantageous way to breathe in many settings, exploring it is beyond the scope of this book.

Feeling good? You're off to a wonderful start! I invite you to make the Belly Breathing Practice a lifelong one. Feel better on all planes—body, mind, emotions and spirit—as a result.

5

Listening To The Sound Of The Breath

The past is history. The future a mystery. This moment is a gift. Which is why it is called "the present".

Are you beginning to understand how pranayama, or the science of breathing, provides potent tools for enhancing and regulating the breath to focus the mind and nourish the body? These benefits unfold as you grow quiet, pause to move awareness into the belly, and establish a relationship with your breath. In doing this, distractions from outside subside and your inner landscape becomes more vivid and real. You are, in essence, resting in the present moment.

Present moment awareness is the doorway to what the ancients refer to as the state of *pratyahara*, or inward abiding.

Where In The World Is Pratyahara?

Pratyahara (pronounced pra-ti-a-hara) is another Sanskrit word, and it means *to turn awareness inward.* As we focus on the rhythm of our breathing, we become less distracted by the world around us. Through that focus, many become better at monitoring their health and well-being, abiding in the experience of solace and serenity. You might too. Belly breathing serves as the foundation for pratyahara, in large part due to its role in minimizing our response to stress.

The time to refine your pranayama practice is after belly breathing has become effortless. Listen to the subtle cues that come from inside you. There are various techniques to consider. Let's play with listening to the breath now.

Tuning In To The Sounds Of The Breath

- When you are ready, remove yourself from distractions as you have already learned to do. Sit in a comfortable position with your spine erect and your shoulders relaxed, and withdraw your awareness from external stimulation. Follow the flow of breath through your nose and let these foundational actions guide your mind inward.
- As you listen inward, imagine that you can hear subtle qualities associated with each portion of the breath. Imagine hearing the inhalation and exhalation whispering inside of you.
- As you focus inward, it may seem as if your breath hums now with little effort, like a well-oiled machine.

Learning to listen to the sound of your breath is a tool that can be used to guide your mind to focus on the inner environment in order to deepen your pranayama journey. When that happens, you may find that you are less buffeted about by the winds of change in the world around you. Slowing down and growing quiet enough to observe the pauses in the breath cycle as well as listen to the sound of the breath is a way to transform breathing from an unconscious act to a transformational art. This process moves us toward meditation, a state more refined and subtle even than pratyahara according to the yogic sages.

What Do You Hear?

What Do You Hear?

It was the rishis, the ancient wisdom-holders from India, who identified the pauses we can distinguish throughout the cycle of breathing and labeled the subtlety of sound we can hear as breath moves in and out of our bodies. Yoga practitioners title this breath practice as the *hamsa breath*, likening the flow of breath to a swan's graceful movements, even on turbulent waters. To one component of the breath, these guides assigned the sound *hum*. To the other they assigned *so*. Listen now and allow the essential sounds of your breath to mature as you practice. Sense into the subtle pauses that exist as well. Imagine the sweet inner sounds that the rishis heard long ago. As you have been learning to do all along the way, please release any effort that you might be making.

Enhance the art of breathing by refining your listening ability. It takes finesse. The trick is to silence the mind and draw awareness inside. As you did when learning the easy breath and belly breathing, please move at a measured pace and adopt a patient attitude while familiarizing yourself with this tool. Relax and savor both the act and the art of conscious breathing.

Why Bother With Pratyahara?

The ancients tell us that pratyahara heightens our sensitivity to the inner environment, providing an opportunity not only to hear the subtle sounds of the breath, but also to harness greater awareness of other elements of ourselves. The sounds associated with the inward and outward flowing breaths have minute differences. For some, this comes across as more of a feeling than a sound.

Regardless of how this manifests for you, listening to the breath is a technique that guides you inward, allowing you to connect with your own inner wisdom, what some call intuition or divine guidance. As you initiate this subtle form of listening, remember to be patient. It is a skill that takes time to develop. Let go of expectations. Appreciate the process and keep in mind what has been said many times already—that the practice becomes easier when you give up effort, approaching it daily and returning to it with the spirit of curiosity and the desire to establish better self-care.

When working with this refined form of inner listening, you may hear, like the rishis did more than five thousand years ago, the subtle sounds of *so* as you inhale and *hum* as you exhale. For some, these sounds are heard in an opposite configuration, *hum* with the inhalation and *so* with the exhalation. Others feel the sounds as a soft vibration. It is possible that you will hear or feel something completely different, or even nothing at all. Remember that the practice will be as unique as you are. There is no right or wrong here. Pratyahara is a way of letting go of judgments about and/or feedback from things that exist outside of you while learning to abide in the peaceful essence at the core of your being—your authentic nature.

Exploring A Mantra Practice

Rather than listening for the sound of *so* and *hum* as you breathe, you could play with assigning your own sounds to the inhalation and exhalation. Once selected, simply repeat them silently as you practice. This is called mantra practice. A mantra, which is a sound, word, or short phrase repeated to aid meditation, is another tool for focusing the mind and eliminating distractions. In Sanskrit, the root *man* refers to the mind, or *manas*. It also means *to think*. The suffix *tra* refers to a tool or instrument. Thus, we might interpret the word to mean *an instrument of the mind*. Some believe that mantras might have been created before formal languages developed. Through the application of a mantra, we learn to rest and center, minimizing the erratic flow of thoughts that often distract us.

If you'd like to try this, play with internally whispering a two-syllable mantra, one syllable as you inhale and one syllable as you exhale. I suggest one of the following: I am, wholeness, peaceful, joyful, happy, loving. As you assign one syllable to each portion of the breath, surrender and let the sounds direct you to the inner landscape. Using mantra with focused breathing will guide you toward the stillness that exists at the center of your being. Slowing down and pausing as you observe the flow of breath into and out of your body may result in a deeply relaxing experience, or even a transformative one.

Points To Remember With Mantra Practice

- Take leisurely, full breaths while your mind repeats one syllable from your chosen phrase as you inhale and one as you exhale. Do this over and over.
- Play with the possibility of pausing ever so slightly between the inhalation and the exhalation phases of breathing.
- Do your best to remain settled and composed as you do this.

Through regular application of this technique, not only are you refining your breathing practice, you are establishing new neural pathways in the brain that may lead to a more prominent sense of overall harmony and well-being in body, mind, and spirit. This has the potential to lead you toward becoming a happier and healthier person. What's not to like about that?

An Antidote To This Esoteric Challenge

Relaxing as you learn to take deeper and slower breaths while simultaneously keeping the mind attentive to inner sounds or a specific word can be challenging. Foster an effortless effort and allow your breathing to nourish and nurture your essential self. In doing so, you may uncover and tap into your true nature. Practice each day. Remember what I've counseled before: it's not the length of time that you work with this in any one session that matters, it's consistency that counts. A little bit goes a long way!

Time For Assessment

Once you've played with the inward-dwelling techniques of pratyahara by listening to the inner sound of your breath for several days or mentally repeating a mantra with the breath, take time out to assess your overall progress. My hope is that you've now established a daily breathing practice that leaves you feeling calm and content.

If the practice of listening to your breath sounds doesn't quite float your boat, you have two choices. You can stay with it a while longer and see if your body/mind adapts or surrenders to the vibration created by the sound. Or you can let it go. While it is a powerful tool for traveling within, even without it, you can still move forward and explore the upcoming breathing and visualization techniques. What's important is to maintain the foundational elements of a breathing practice—the easy breath and belly breathing—while building up the length of time you practice.

Sitting quietly and breathing with awareness for ten to fifteen minutes each day, or even longer, has numerous benefits. Notice how you feel both during the practice and also throughout the day. Are there any changes in the way that you engage with the world around you? You're doing good work. Keep it up!

6

Modulating The Breath

When you arise in the morning, think of what
a precious privilege it is to be alive—
to breathe, to think, to enjoy, to love.
-Marcus Aurelius

By now, you've done the hard work of mastering two important practices: the Easy Breath and Belly Breathing. With those as a foundation, we will explore when to artfully enjoy an easy, balanced breath and when to extend one segment of it or the other in order to bring about specific results. There has been no restriction applied to your breath flow at this point, only an *allowing* of these unique actions to occur. Now you may build upon these actions, learning how to modulate the breath in specific ways to enhance relaxation. Many have successfully applied the following tools to mitigate stress and elevate levels of patience and joy.

Counting The Breath

Bringing oxygen (and prana) into the body, the inhalation has energizing qualities. The exhalation, in contrast, offers a chance to let go. Knowing this, one may choose to lengthen the rate of either part of the breath to energize or to release stress and relax. The cornerstone of this is a Balanced Breath Practice, which occurs when air is taken in and released out at an even rate. We come to this practice and build on it by learning to count the breath. As I've said before, understanding comes through practice. Do your best to apply a smooth and effortless belly breath all the way through as you explore the variations on counting the breath, which follow.

Establishing A Balanced Breath

- Prepare for equal breathing with three effortless rounds of belly breathing.
- Then continue belly breathing as you silently count along during the out-breath each time you exhale. Perform these actions two or three times to get an average count.
- Mentally note the rate at which you are releasing breath. Your exhalation may last for a count of four, five, six, or something else. Remember that number.
- Next, modulate the rate at which you inhale so that it lasts for the same count as your exhalation. This results in a balanced breath.
- After several repetitions of a Balanced Breath Practice, pause to note how you feel. This harmonious way of breathing heightens energy levels for some people. It creates a more consistent mental and/or emotional state for others. A few people feel lightheaded initially. If you do feel lightheaded, know that this should subside over time as you continue to practice in a calm and gentle

manner. Give yourself plenty of time to adjust to the practice and to the greater balance in the gases you are exchanging. What is your experience?

Like the other breathing tools, counting the breath is effective in part because it turns the mind away from possible sources of irritation or anxiety. Because of that, it may offer instant stress relief.

Counting the breath to establish a balanced breath, as you have just learned how to do, is a wonderful tool for quelling the ambitions of a restless mind, as are each of the practices you've explored to this point. These techniques work, in part, because they require you to pay attention to how you breathe. As that becomes effortless, you build an outstanding platform from which to examine—more deeply—how breathing well contributes to living well. In times of stress, your breath rate changes. Balanced Breathing Practice gives you a tool that may counter this. It serves to guide your mind and/or emotional state back into an experience of harmony and equilibrium. From that place, you are better equipped to navigate fluctuating states of activity with grace.

Easy Does It. 1,2,3,4… 1,2,3,4…

Explore The Pause

If you like this and want to take the practice further, implement counting through each of the four portions of the breath cycle. In other words, count not only during inhalation and exhalation, but also during the pauses between them too. For starters, allow your pauses to last for half as long as you breathe in or out. Please remember that pausing is not the same thing as holding the breath. A pause may feel as if you are still inhaling or exhaling but without air coming in or leaving. You do not want to hold your breath if you suffer from any illness or disease, particularly if you have eye trouble, anxiety, or cancer. Consider the pauses as extensions of inhalation and exhalation. They are the space that the breath needs to turn itself around. They provide an opportunity to release *doing* and settle into *being*, if only temporarily. Remain calm with muscles relaxed as you practice.

The analogy shared by one of my colleagues was that of making a bed. Imagine tossing a clean and lightweight sheet up into the air as you spread it out over the bed. It hovers slightly in the air before falling effortlessly downward. It may hover on the bed, too, before you toss it out one more time to straighten it.

The basic approach is as follows:

- ➢ Breathe out for a specific count—four, five, or six—then pause, abiding in the stillness of an empty state while mentally counting to two or three.

- Breathe in for the same count as you breathed out (four, five or six). Then pause again for two or three counts. Continue this pattern for as long as you'd like.
- Gradually, and only if you are in complete health in body, mind, and emotions, allow your pauses to grow longer. If it feels good and if it seems beneficial, the pauses may grow to last as long as your inhalation and exhalation, but it is not necessary to extend them that long.

Just as you have with other breathing practices, I want you to inhale and exhale slowly and smoothly to maintain a sense of calm repose as you count. Pause after the inhalation to appreciate the full-of-breath state and absorb prana while transitioning toward your exhale breath. Pause following the exhalation to enjoy a sense of non-doing and lingering rest. Many comment on how they feel more alive, more animated and alert after a few rounds of this four-part balanced breathing activity.

Once you are comfortable with the Balanced Breath Practice and are ready to explore additional ways to modulate your breathing, please continue. What follows are tools you can employ for specific reasons. Belly breathing is foundational to them, and they build on counting the breath.

Lengthening Only The Exhalation

- Relief from stress comes by breathing out because the exhalation functions like a release valve. Not only does it carry carbon dioxide and other waste materials out from the body, helping to balance the pH of the body, it allows us to discharge built-up tension. To benefit, I invite you to explore this now by lengthening the rate at which you exhale. The format is similar to counting the breath, except that the rate of your inhalation remains steady while your exhalation grows longer over the course of several breaths.
- Count your breath for several rounds and establish a balanced breath with an even rate for each portion of it.
- Maintain this rate for your inhalation and gradually but deliberately lengthen the exhalation over the course of several breaths.

- Each time you breathe out, slow down your exhalation. Stretch it out. With practice, you may find that it lingers and becomes twice as long as your inhalation. The natural pause after the exhalation may become longer as well. Notice and allow rather than force.
- The result may be that you are breathing in a pattern much like 4-4-8-4 or 4-4-8-8. Continue this pattern five or six times before letting it go, breathing naturally, and observing the effects. Many report heightened relaxation. Do you?

Manipulating The Breath Count For Specific Reasons

Slowing down the exhalation has the potential to calm and cleanse you, helping release the cellular by-products of stress from the body. In contrast, lengthening the inhalation can serve as an energetic pick-me-up by bringing more oxygen in. You are in the driver's seat when you engage with these breathing practices. It doesn't take many rounds of any of these modulations to benefit from them.

Once you know how to modulate the breath by either lengthening the exhalation or the inhalation, you have powerful tools that can be used as part of an ongoing practice or can be used when particular life circumstances call for a secret weapon. And modulating the breath is a powerful secret weapon.

7

The Mountain Breath

On the mountains of truth you can never climb in vain: either you will reach a point higher up today, or you will be training your powers so that you will be able to climb higher tomorrow.

-Friedrich Nietzsche

If you have become comfortable with the practices discussed up to this point, you are ready to take on the final pranayama practice. I have labeled it fondly the Mountain Breath. This technique, which is another option for modulating your breath with specific intent, is a variation of the ancient practice of *Nadi Shodana*, also known as alternate nostril breathing. It builds on all of the previous practices and may help you summit the metaphorical mountains in your life.

The Mountain Breath Practice is a wonderful stress-relieving tool that can energize and revitalize you when you are feeling dull or lethargic and bring you to center when the stresses of the day leave you feeling scattered or anxious. Belly breathing and balanced breathing form the base of the Mountain Breath Practice. They also support it. Among its many benefits, Mountain Breath Practice is effective at integrating the two hemispheres of the brain, strengthening the lungs, and balancing the energies in the body. Take your time learning to breathe through alternate nostrils. Once you have learned the practice, you just might find yourself employing it when you are stopped at a traffic light, before you enter an important meeting, or before you go to bed. It calms and centers body, mind, and emotions. Its application is endless; it's benefits, tremendous.

Some Interesting Facts

I call this practice the Mountain Breath because, to me, the visual is much like that of walking up one side of a mountain and down the other (again, and again, and again). The benefits of mountain breathing come from the way we move air through the nostrils in an alternating pattern. Breathing through the left nostril stimulates the parasympathetic nervous system, the rest and digest system. Breathing through the right nostril stimulates the sympathetic nervous system, the fight, flight, or freeze system. Stimulating the left nostril calms and cools. Simulating the right nostril stirs up the cardiovascular system and body thermostat. By alternating breaths through each nostril, these energies become harmonious and integrated, allowing a sense of steadiness and balance to wash through you after practicing the breath technique.

Find Your Way Up The Mountain

- As with the other practices, minimize distraction and sit comfortably with spine erect and shoulders relaxed in preparation for Mountain Breath Practice. Then take three breaths all the way in through both nostrils and release them all the way out through the mouth with an audible sigh, bringing your awareness into the present moment.

- Establish belly breathing while breathing in a comfortably deep, restful, and soothing manner. Let these qualities set the tone for your mountain climbing experience.
- Now, steady your awareness on the breath and imagine breathing out only through the left nostril. Then imagine taking air in through the left nostril.
- As the breath enters the body through the left nostril, visualize it moving up toward the center of the brain. Then pause, allowing prana to saturate the brain with life-enhancing and healing energy.
- The exhalation will move out the right nostril. As you exhale, imagine breath traveling downward and out only through the right nostril. Then pause in an empty-of-breath state for a moment.
- Now breathe in and up into the brain through the right nostril. Pause before releasing it down and out the left nostril to complete one round of Mountain Breath Practice.
- Implementing this pattern over and over—breathing in left, out right, in right, and out left—is how we alternate

the nostrils through which air travels. For me, the visual is much like walking up and down a mountain.

- Do this in balanced fashion, breathing in and out at the same rate, to enhance the action of this practice.
- Allow your mind to follow the breath and notice the pauses while simultaneously imagining prana saturating the brain with each breath. You might begin with a 4-2-4-2 pattern. Extend the pauses so that the pattern eventually becomes 4-4-4-4 only if the breath technique continues to be a calming and pleasant experience.
- Please note that the simple act of visualizing this pattern, as opposed to mechanically closing and opening each nostril (which I explain later), works very well. It is just as powerful as the physical manipulation of the nostrils.

Enjoy A Leisurely Stroll

The Mountain Breath is a soothing and gentle way to elevate your practice as you get the hang of it, and you do not want to rush through it. Let it serve as a stand-alone practice or layer it over other pranayama techniques. Choose the mountain breath for its ability to establish steadiness and equanimity, which can assist you in summiting the metaphorical peaks of life with alacrity and joy.

As you make that leisurely stroll, here are a few things to help you fine-tune your climb:

- Imagine each time you breathe in through one nostril that you are joyfully and effortlessly ascending the mountain of the mind. Just as easily, when you breathe out the opposite nostril you travel down the other side of the mountain. Some folks *see* this with the mind's eye. Others *feel* it. Use whatever sensory modality works for you.
- Keep your mind focused on the flow of breath in and out through the nose. As breath (and awareness) enters one nostril, imagine it moving up into the middle of the brain as you inhale. Then imagine it traveling down and out the second nostril with the exhalation. After that, you will breathe in through the second side (the side you just finished exhaling through) and out again through

the first side (the side you first inhaled through). That completes one round of Mountain Breath Practice.

- I suggest applying one to three rounds of the technique a few times a day for several days until it becomes familiar. Then you can add another round to your practice each day until you have built up to fivc minutes or more of mountain breathing as a regular practice.
- To end the practice, pause after your final exhalation out the left nostril. Then take a smooth, full breath in through both nostrils again. Breath naturally through both nostrils again from this point on.
- Take time to soak up the results of this soothing and balancing form of breath modulation after you finish.

Let one to three rounds of Mountain Breath Practice serve as your first practice, after which you will rest while breathing naturally through both nostrils. Feel free to increase the number of rounds as you become absorbed by the rapture of this activity. Because the mountain breath is so beneficial, you are welcome to implement a few rounds of it throughout the day as needed to promote tranquility.

A Mudra May Help

For some, using their fingers to alternately close the nostrils establishes a more tangible connection to this breath practice due to the physical aspect of guiding the breath. A light touch is all that's needed. The right hand is used to do this while the left hand rest comfortably on the arm of your chair or in your lap, or is used to count the number of repetitions you are practicing if you are interested in keeping track of them. Using the hand in this way is a form of mudra, or ritual hand position. Use this outline to practice working with the mudra:

- Form a mudra by raising your right hand, palm facing your face. Fold the first two fingers (index and middle fingers) in toward the palm.
- Breathe in through both nostrils and then gently rest your thumb over the right nostril. Very light pressure is all that is needed to close it off, allowing you to breathe out the left nostril, and then to take air in only through the left nostril.

- Pause after inhaling through your left nostril, release the soft thumb pressure from your right nostril and close the left nostril now using a soft press of the ring finger of the same hand.
- Breathe out through the right nostril. Then keep the right nostril open and breathe in through it. Pause. Then close the right nostril with a light press of the thumb and breathe out through the left nostril to complete one round of the Mountain Breath.
- After a brief pause, implement this again for round two. *Breathe in left, out right. In Right, out left.* Your actions should smooth out as you release effort and settle into the flow of breath moving from one nostril to the other and back again.
- Do this one more time for a third round, then let the practice go for now and breathe naturally through both nostrils, as you cultivate awareness of how you feel.

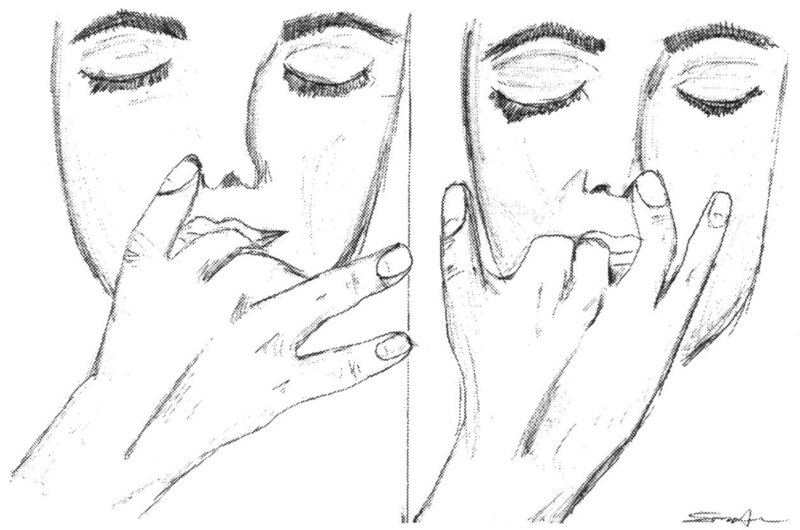

Apply Vishnu Mudra With Your Right Hand.

Points Of Interest Along The Mountain

There is no need to rush your mountain climb. The pauses between the in and out breath serve you well here. Each time you breathe in, imagine slowly ascending the mountain. Pause and imagine turning around, preparing for your descent.

Each time you breathe out, imagine a slow and delightful trip down the other side of the mountain. Pause again to rest naturally before drawing another breath in and journeying up the mountain again. By doing this, the energy that you expend will be minimal, and your breathing will become a pleasurable activity. Slowing your pace and merging with the process makes the practice of this breath sublime, as does practicing with regularity.

As your familiarity with the practice increases, build up the number of rounds you implement over the course of several days. Practicing mountain breath should leave you feeling relaxed, alert, and more balanced than before you started. As the mind becomes occupied by observing the flow of breath through each nostril, the practice may easily evolve into a meditation. That is when you know you have effectively turned inward and can abide in a place of deep and universal wisdom.

Harmony Is The Result

As mentioned before, the mountain breath is a specific pranayama tool used to harmonize and integrate the two hemispheres of the brain and balance the two parts of the autonomic nervous system. Through its application, the entire nervous system is invited to rest and the mind is encouraged to quiet. A sense of balance and tranquility may wash over the whole of your being while clarity and concentration increase. This breathing modality also presents a simple remedy for acute stress. In fact, the soothing nature of this practice makes it suitable for alleviating any situation that has the potential for being stressful. A friend of mine shared that she engaged with mountain breath in the waiting room each time her husband went in for his cancer treatments. It helped her to remain calm and hopeful during a worrisome time. Climb the mountain and take in the gorgeous and life affirming views that await you!

8

Honoring Emotions

The best and most beautiful things in the

world cannot be seen or even touched.

They must be felt with the heart.

-Helen Keller

My hope is that by this time you have experienced how conscious breathing brings about good feelings. The process doesn't take much time. Yet there may be times when an unfamiliar emotion arises due to the movement of awareness deeper into the body. If your habitual pattern is to shut down or disassociate from feelings, conscious breathing can give you a new option—and an effective one—for working with emotions.

When you can keep breathing as emotion arises, taking comfortably long, comfortably deep breaths in and letting them out smoothly while observing the changes that come to your mood and to the moment, you will soon find that the emotion has subsided. You're sure to land on the other side of it this way. I liken it to skiing down a steep and slippery mountain slope or riding a wild and curving roller coaster. Eventually, both activities come to completion. Practicing breathing in calm moments allows you to navigate both the challenges and the pleasures of life as they arise with a greater sense of ease.

Even if you are not a skier, imagine what it would be like if you traveled straight down a steep slope without stopping along the way. Most likely, you would continue to accelerate and quite possibly end up skiing too fast for comfort and out of control. Worry and even fear might overtake your mind to the point that your breathing would be the last thing you would consider.

Contrast that with imagining that you are starting out more slowly and pausing along the way to make some turns and notice the scenery in a leisurely, pleasant way. Your awareness of your breathing continues during that unhurried trip down the mountain, and you notice that you are able to maintain a smooth, even breath through your nose as you ski. This does wonders for your entire experience.

By consistently applying breathing practices to your day-to-day life and refining them as you go, the steadiness you cultivate informs other aspects of your life, too. You learn to discern when to modulate your breath versus when to let go of control, and that awareness influences your actions and may enhance your activities and relationships, too.

The desire to manage or control experience is quite strong in many people. If you've parented teenagers, raised a dog, or lived with roommates, you've most likely realized that to maintain a positive relationship, there's a time to exert control in the form of discipline or stern communication, and a time to go with the flow. It's the same with breath practice. As you befriend your breath by bringing more awareness to it, my guess is that you'll be able to negotiate change with grace and more confidently field the curve balls that life throws your way.

Harmonizing The Messengers That Live Within Us

I've said this before: strong emotions may surface when you start taking fuller breaths. If the feelings that arise have been suppressed for some time, they will likely have lodged into your body. Many of us did not have the tools or time to explore feelings now deeply suppressed when we first experienced them, or we did explore them but in a way that directed our attention to the cause of the feeling rather than the feeling itself. If the cause was a stressful situation or pressing obligation that seemed to need immediate attention, we might have subverted our feeling response to it.

Those behaviors are natural. By priming us to fight, flee, or freeze in conflictual situations, the stress response readies the body for action, not for processing our experience. At those times, blood is shunted from the interior of the body to the periphery, fueling our legs and arms. As we have already learned, digestion, emotion, and circulation to the organs within the torso are restricted when we operate from this stressfully aroused state. One result of this is a buildup of fat around the belly because as stressful conditions persist, they signal to the body that it may needed additional resources in the form of calories to burn as it pushes through.

There was a time when that bodily reaction kept us safe and there was adequate time for recovery in a safe place after the threat was gone. But nowadays, with full schedules and the unending stimulation of a busy life, the stress response goes into overdrive. Without factoring time into each day to pause and relax, emotion, pain, and strain are not easily released. Instead, they burrow into the body, leading to disease. Breathing into an uncomfortable feeling, memory, or experience helps one let it go. This keeps us healthy in the long run.

Mindful breathing offers the chance to release negative buildup in a gentle and effective manner. If you are able to continue breathing smoothly and deeply all the way through an arising emotion, the emotion has a chance to surface, move through, and release rather than become lodged deeper within you. Consider your emotions to be the moguls on a ski slope, the ups and downs on the roller coaster of life, the waves on an ocean. If you can maintain a relatively smooth and easy breath as you negotiate those ups and downs, your experiences and reactions to stress do ultimately level out. The bumpy ride eventually ends.

With awareness, you may even tip your experience into a more pleasant place. A wonderful benefit of establishing a regular, steady, and nourishing breath practice is that it serves to minimize the highs and lows of our emotional response to all that goes on around us. The result is that life becomes more stable and consistent, more peaceful. Your heart may open as your mind grows quiet, allowing you to experience and express a full range of emotions as you respond with greater levels of wisdom and compassion for all you encounter.

Allowing Emotions To Surface And Dissipate

If you're willing, use your breath practice to explore letting emotions surface rather than stifling them or cutting them off. Allow any tears that arise to flow. By carving out a space and a time to explore the breathing practices offered in this book, my hope is that you will grow to feel safe contemplating all that springs up during your practice. With time, you may find that you become more skilled at breathing your way into and through the variety of changing experiences you encounter in any given day. Doing your best to breathe with awareness all the way through a stressful experience not only helps to release what has been stored in the body, but also helps to integrate it. Our tendency is to hold our breath when we are scared or tense. But by remembering to keep breathing and having an established breath practice to rely on, the body tenses less and the mind remains clearer and more focused, enabling one to artfully dance through many a challenging situation.

Breathing through stress prevents it from lodging in the body and even facilitates the release of any negative response to it. After all, stress is simply a message that your thoughts and actions are out of alignment with what's happening around you. Take a moment to pause. Take a deep breath in and sigh it out slowly as you assess the situation. Then continue belly breathing and you will move through the situation in less time than it takes to fill your car with gas.

Honoring emotions requires you to pause instead of automatically suppressing or blasting past them. When you pause after inhalation, every cell is nourished because prana is absorbed. When you pause after exhalation, you cultivate a moment of peaceful non-doing.

This, in and of itself, leads to a state of union with all things and with nothing at the same time. That is the value of this subtle, yet very important forth stage of the breath cycle.

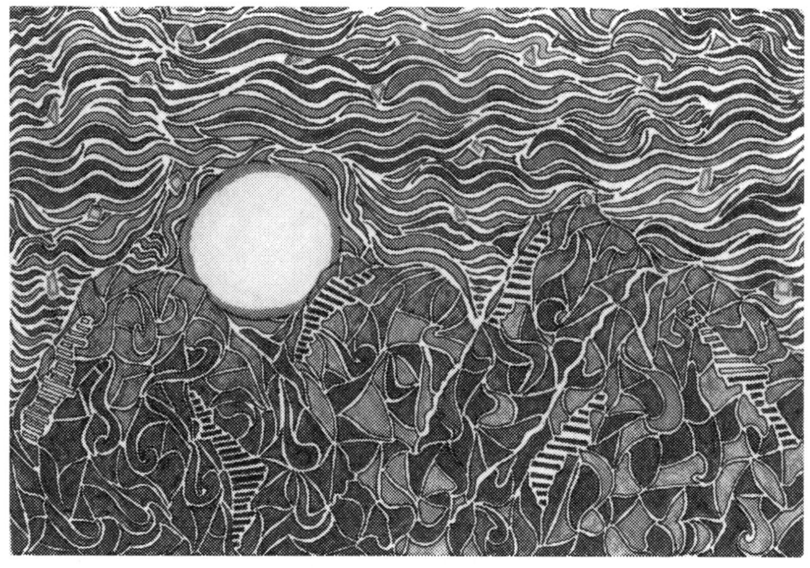

Aware. Fluid. Integrated. One with the Elements of Nature.

Breathing through your emotions is one way of honoring them. And like almost anything else in life, when they are honored, they lose their potential for becoming an enemy and instead become a respected part of life. With that, life becomes more present moment oriented and fluid, and we become more comfortable with it.

9

Imagine The Possibilities

Accept what is in front of you, without wanting the situation to be other than it is. Nature provides everything, without requiring thanks and provides for all.

-Lao Tzu

The honoring of emotions, as just discussed, requires you to pause and inquire into their source instead of automatically suppressing or ignoring them. When you pause after inhalation, every cell is nourished because prana is absorbed. When you pause after exhalation, you are allowing for a moment of peaceful non-doing. I encourage you to explore how this might connect you to all things.

In the state of non-doing, you are primed to experience the results of an additional mindfulness technique, Creative Visualization Practice. While it may be applied as an alternative to your breathing practice, using the easy breath and belly breathing simultaneously makes this practice more effective.

Did you know that creative visualization has been shown to increase relaxation and focus as well as reduce the sense of lingering stress, acute and chronic pain, and anxiety? Visualizing a peaceful setting can even help to lower blood pressure. Parents in my mindful parenting classes use visualization—seeing their children as the beautiful beings they know them to be—to navigate parenting challenges better, too. I invite you to give visualization a try.

The tools of the imagination have been used since ancient times not only to outline and manifest goals, but also to support emotional release. In fact, they work so well that the skills of imagery have been applied by people in diverse settings to maximize results. Talented athletes use visualization to win Olympic events. Business executives apply it to win important contracts. People who want to win at relationship building with their children, partners, friends, and themselves use it. While some people believe that we need to go to battle to win, the perspective I have proposed throughout this book is that by disengaging or letting go and taking time to rest and breathe well, we feel happier and our health improves. Combine that with time spent visualizing the life you desire and I suggest that you will be winning at lifc.

The two practices in this chapter, The Body Scan and The Tropical Vacation Guided Meditation, involve visualization. You use your mind to facilitate relaxation and to imagine what is being suggested while exploring the tension housed in the body. Like the breathing tools, these two techniques are great for alleviating stress. Their effectiveness is elevated when added to an already established breathing practice. Adding these imagery practices at least once a week to your daily breathing practice is a good way to even further enhance the equanimity you have been developing. I encourage you to either record these visualizations for your own use or contact me for a free downloadable recording of them.

The Body Scan

This is a practice of focusing the mind and moving awareness through the body, seeking pockets of tension or unnecessary holding. When you encounter tension, imagine it melting away as you breathe. Much like snow melts from a mountaintop under the summer sun, you can visualize tension melting out of the body as you scan through it. Imagine you can breathe into any tight areas you find. Use the prana coming in as you inhale to open up these tight areas and the exhalation to carry the tightness and tension away. The pauses may be used to evaluate the practice to note if there is any more tension to release.

- Remove yourself from distractions. Sit quietly with your spine erect, shoulders relaxed, seat rooted into the chair beneath you, and feet on the floor (or alternatively rest completely supported by the floor or your bed). Initiate belly breathing.
- Take your awareness to the top of your head. Imagine that you can breathe into and out of this location for several breaths. Sense this area softening and expanding with each breath.

- Guide your awareness (your mind) downward from the top of the head into each and every part below. Move slowly. Mindfully explore the parts of your face. Your forehead. Your temples, out to the ears. The bridge of your nose. The tip of your nose. Your jaw. Your mouth, your tongue, your throat. Take awareness into your neck and shoulders. Location by location, seek any tightness that exists and imagine it releasing each time you exhale. Give yourself plenty of time to do this.
- Let go. As you discover any unnecessary holding or tension, mentally and physically let it go. Remember that the inhalation opens up tight areas and the exhalation releases what is no longer needed.
- Now scan your shoulders, chest, and upper back. Any tension there? Let it go.
- Move awareness down your arms and into your hands. Are your fingers open or closed? Are you palms upright or facing downward? Do your arms rest comfortably or would they like some support?
- Become aware of your ribs now. Imagine the spaces between them growing wider as you inhale and gently

narrowing as you exhale. Imagine the cage they form around your heart and lungs. Allow it to expand slightly with each inhalation. It softens as you exhale. Imagine the organs in your chest relaxing, too.

- Become aware of your middle and lower back. Allow this area of your body to become more spacious now. Release any tension you hold there over the course of several breaths.
- Take awareness into your belly. Soften the belly. Let it move with each breath. Breathe in and out with awareness centered in your belly, the organs receiving a light massage as you breathe.
- Now move awareness into your pelvis. Soften and relax through this part of your body. Take awareness out into your hips, down your legs, around your knees, and through your feet.
- Soften and let go as you travel through the body.
- Remain as long as necessary in any tight spots you find as you scan your body, and imagine that you could breathe into and out of specific locations.

- Use the body scan to sense into every part of your body while breathing consciously. Move your awareness down through all the parts of your body, bringing the awareness of the mind into the body and grounding the energy of the body into the earth. Continue with this body scan practice for as long as you would like.
- Upon completion, pause. Notice what changed since before you began the body scan. Take a moment to appreciate the stillness and relaxation that may have resulted.

Consider these questions: Do you noticc a change in how you feel now compared to before you did the Body Scan? What was your experience of the Body Scan Practice? Journaling about it is a helpful way to track and process what you notice as you work with this practice over time. Some people sense a message lodged in a particular part of the body as they learn to bring their awareness to that part of the body. Did you? If so, as you return a sense of loving awareness to that space over the course of several practices, a message may emerge or a pain may erode away. What is left behind is a sense of spaciousness and ease where tenderness or even significant discomfort once sat.

If you are new to this practice, the challenges are in focusing your mind on each part of the body and in moving slowly enough to root out tension. Nonetheless, it is a great way to enhance your relationship with your physical body over time, and it is yet another tool for soothing and focusing the mind. Like the breathing practices, The Body Scan Practice can be used to release tightness in the body and free emotions that have become trapped in a particular location. When that happens, whether it happens consciously or unconsciously, you may find that you feel freer and experience heightened levels of joy and unbridled happiness at random moments throughout the day.

Consider applying a lengthy and luxurious body scan regularly. It may be something you come to in place of or in addition to your regular breathing practice at least once a week. Feel free to use a quick version of it more often as time allows. If you ever feel unsettled with this practice, please seek out the support of a yoga therapist, stress management educator, or other complementary health care provider. There is no reason to put up with uncomfortable feelings or sensations for very long.

The Tropical Vacation Guided Meditation

You may enjoy this guided mediation either seated or lying down. Once settled into a quiet space where you are sure to remain uninterrupted for a time, please bring to mind a beautiful tropical ocean. Imagine one that is calm and tranquil. The warm, salty water is a delightful turquoise blue color and very clear. As you gaze into it, you see small rainbow-colored fish swimming harmoniously just under the surface of the water and pink seashells scattered on the sandy bottom. Imagine the rhythmic sound of the waves as they gently and continuously flow onto the shore and wash effortlessly back into the broad, beautiful, warm, tranquil ocean.

Imagine how serene and peaceful this location is and how you feel drawn to rest on the warm, sandy beach for a while. Visualize yourself sitting down on the beach near the blue water, perhaps on a colorful towel or blanket. The sand around you is a lovely golden color. Notice how the sand feels both soft and firm beneath you. Both the sand and the air around you are just the right temperature. The whole setting calls you to relax as you sit there on a pleasantly warm and cloudless day, listening to the rhythmic sound of the waves.

A flock of pelicans flies overhead. You hear the soft pressure of their wings against the air as they fly. A cool breeze carries the scent of salt water on it. Contrast the coolness of the breeze with the warmth of the sunlight that shines down on your skin. The rays of sunlight are soft, not harsh. Imagine that they are releasing gentle, healing energy. Their warmth penetrates all the tight areas of your body.

Imagine that you can allow the healing, tension-relieving warmth of the sunlight to saturate your body as you sit contentedly on the sandy beach, gazing out over the calm, blue sea. Visualize yourself as peaceful and rested as you pause in this serene environment. Now notice that sunlight sparkles on the tips of the gentle waves out in the ocean. Beyond that, at the horizon stretches a vast, blue sky. Nearby there's a musical sound as the breeze lightly rustles the leaves of palm trees. All is well. You are satisfied, rested, and feel joy in your heart.

Now wiggle your toes. Wiggle them into the glorious sand beneath them until your feet are covered by it. The tiny grains of silky, golden sand collect around your feet as you nestle them into it. Any tension or pain that existed in your feet before this moment melts away as you enjoy the comfortable cocooning sensation of the sand pooling around them.

Imagine the possibility of letting all cares go. Imagine feeling completely safe, calm, and peaceful surrounded by this tropical paradise. For a bit longer, visualize the waves sweetly pulling stress and strain away from you as you linger on the beach of the mind.

As you do this, pause. Invite qualities of safety, serenity, and present moment awareness to inform your experience. End the visualization when you feel ready to do so by returning your awareness to your breath and to its gentle flow in and out through your nose.

Then bring awareness to sensations in your body. Eventually become aware of the room around you. Pause to integrate the relaxing feeling cultivated during this meditation.

Before transitioning from this guided meditation back into the obligations of your life, I encourage you to express gratitude. Gratitude is the fertilizer of our dreams. Acknowledge how you feel after taking a brief, mental tropical vacation from a secluded spot in your home or office. Take a moment to appreciate the experience, and to feel grateful for the chance to take a time out.

Consider carrying some of the peaceful feelings that developed during the meditation with you into the rest of your day or night. They are there for you and available any time you care to access them. Please know that you can add to this visualization in any way, and you can linger with it for as long as you have time. Use it as a temporary retreat from a hectic day or as a way to unwind before you retire for the night.

Potent Life Tools

Both the Body Scan Practice and the Tropical Vacation Guided Meditation are potent tools for alleviating stress. Engage with them for as briefly or as long as your time allows. Apply them when you need a break or when you feel tight, tired, or tenuous about a situation. By training your attention on experiences or thoughts that feel good, you may be able to release those that distract you from the harmony of life. In this way, we let go of the need to be busy; let go of the to-do list and let stuck emotion flow.

As mindful breathing does, both The Body Scan and the Tropical Vacation Guided Meditation bring us into the present moment. A busy mind along with a nonstop schedule of duties and obligations keep us on the hamster wheel of life, often stuck in memories of the past or worried about the future. Only through present moment awareness can we release ourselves from that. It is in the present that healing is available to us. When you let go of what you cannot control right now, release what no longer serves you, and rest in *this* moment, you are living your life and learning to thrive.

Learn to breathe, learn to rest, and learn to allow yourself to flow with life. These will come together as potent tools for living a full and wonderful life.

10

Putting It All Together

I don't think much of one who isn't wiser

today than he was yesterday.

-Abraham Lincoln

Connect. Reflect. Implement. If you have made it this far, you are well on your way to stimulating awareness of your body/mind and experiencing enhanced well-being on all levels. All of the individual tools found here can be implemented individually or combined together. And they may be used as often as you choose to address specific situations. Take license to use them as you are called to, forming a dynamic and healing daily practice.

My own breathing practice has been a trusted companion for many years, allowing me to remain connected to my inner voice as I have navigated the challenges of parenting and building a business designed to serve those seeking steadiness in a tumultuous world. It is my hope that you, too, will grow to enjoy these practices and the benefits they offer, and that you will choose to implement them with regularity and joy. In doing so, you will be taking care of what matters, strengthening your inner resolve, and bringing your best self into all you do. This will allow you to engage with work and relationships from a place of truth and authenticity.

A Guide To An Integrated Practice

- ➢ Solidify and strengthen your intention to establish a potent personal practice by attending to your practice at the same time and in the same place every day. Assure that you will be uninterrupted for at least ten to twenty minutes each day.
- ➢ Position yourself in a relaxed yet upright posture by sitting with an erect spine, soft shoulders, and heavy

bottom (like the sand that spreads out over the base of an hourglass when it is newly tipped). Anchor your energy down through the base of your body. Then take two or three deep breaths in and actively sigh them out through your mouth to release tension and bring yourself into the present moment.

- Establish an easy breath and initiate belly breathing, welcoming movement in your belly as you breathe through your nose.
- Perhaps scan your body briefly at this point to notice if you harbor unnecessary tension. Rotate your awareness through your body while letting your mind guide the energy of the breath into any pockets of tension you find. Give the tension or resistance you encounter permission to soften and even melt away for the time being. Visualize your inhalation opening tight areas. Release any unnecessary holding each time you exhale.
- After the body scan, return awareness to your breathing and to the movements in your belly. Remain focused on that for a short practice of five or ten more minutes

before ending with a brief expression of gratitude for all you have and all that your practice brings to you.

- Alternatively, spend more time with the belly breathing and/or body scan, letting that set a soothing tone for a longer practice.
- If time allows, choose one or two additional tools to apply. This might be one of the pratyahara practices like listening for the internal sound of the breath or mentally repeating a couple of short words or syllables each time you inhale and exhale.
- Another option is to work only with the mountain breath by taking breaths in and out softly through alternate nostrils for as long as seems beneficial and ending with a natural breath through both nostrils while you pause to savor the experience.
- Using the tools in these ways constitutes a beneficial and integrated practice that can be applied for fifteen to twenty minutes or longer every day. Appreciate its ability to melt tension from your body while quieting and focusing your mind.

- As you near the end of your practice, take time to appreciate the peace you feel within you. You are welcome to linger in this serene state for as long as you remain comfortable and content.
- Before ending your practice, silently repeat words of gratitude for your practice and for the time you are able to carve out of your day to connect with your breath. Acknowledge how life force energy has the ability to support and nourish your whole being and connect you to everything around you.
- You are now ready to move with ease into the rest of your day or to settle into a restful sleep.

Reminders For A Satisfying Practice

I hope it's clear that there is nothing to seek as you establish a constructive daily practice. All you are being asked to do is slow down and pay attention. Combine that with a letting go of the need to achieve anything specific, if only for minutes every day, and watch your health and well-being improve in subtle yet everlasting ways. Put another way, by tuning into the subtleties of breathing as a life-giving act, we fill ourselves up, both literally and figuratively. Not only do we feel better, we also have more energy and attention to give others. And our interactions with the world around us become an outpouring of the love that comes from caring for ourselves. It is in this way that we bring our best self forward into all that we do.

Please know that when you take time out of what may seem to be a very busy day to practice breathing, you are giving yourself a gift. You are setting yourself up for a successful day if you practice in the morning, and you are preparing for a restful sleep if you practice at night. You are also connecting with the web of life. The positive, life-affirming energy that travels with the breath is available to all of us, and it permeates the entire planet. As you allow and even invite more of this universal life force energy to flow through you as you release tight muscles and tension throughout the body, not only does this energy flow into you, it also flows from you to others. Your practice benefits both you and others. This is something that has to be experienced to be understood. Why wait?

Begin today! Covet the time that you set aside on a daily basis to do nothing more than sit and breathe. May you find the act of breathing to be a playful experience and a practice that you look forward to experiencing most every day. When we breathe better, we live better. What's not to like about that?

A Wonderful Paradigm Shift

The practice of breathing may take getting used to because it creates a paradigm shift. In my work as a holistic stress management educator and yoga therapist, I look at the whole instead of addressing the parts when I consider methods to enhance well-being and joy. I look at the whole individual and how that individual fits into the world around her.

As forms of complementary health care, holistic stress management and yoga therapy offer similar approaches to personal development and wellness that refreshingly counter the Western medical model. They invite us to shift our view away from looking at the parts (which include physical health, mental health, emotional health, and spiritual health) that comprise an individual and gaze instead upon the whole being to facilitate healing. Instead of focusing only on what is not working or what is wrong with an individual or situation, we consider what is out of whack or what might be missing and what is needed to make a situation or individual whole. From a sense of being scattered comes integration. From the integration of body, mind (as both intellect and emotion), and spirit comes healing. The question isn't so much what needs to be fixed. Instead, we consider how to enhance what's already working, taking a long-term view to overall health. We use breath to transform stress in ways that beneficially impact ones overall health and happiness.

As Jon Kabat-Zinn says in his book *Full Catastrophe Living*, healing involves an attitudinal and emotional transformation. Breath work and visualization are both powerful tools that facilitate this transformation. Each of them can be refined or enhanced to address specific situations, and both can be relied on to find your way back to the center of your being. Consider them as the hub of life and your feelings, actions, thoughts, and behaviors as the spokes.

If you consider a circle, without beginning or end, and divide that into four equal parts, it represents the wholeness I am describing. The four parts represent the physical, mental, emotional, and spiritual selves. Each piece, each component of the whole, influences and plays a vital role in your health and well-being. These pieces combine in a personal wellness paradigm to strengthen and support individual health. They influence planetary health, as well. Distributing your energy and awareness between them facilitates a balanced life, and a balanced life is important to both personal and planetary health.

Given that the individual is a microcosm of the universal, balanced living begets wholeness. It's the amalgamation of the parts that facilitates wholeness and provides an opportunity for relief from the stress that pulls things apart. Through intention and integration, the stress that diminishes us can be distributed between the parts, and thus minimized.

When your body is in pain, breathe into the pain. When your mind is racing or dull, change up the way you breathe to counter that. As emotions surface—be they anger, fear, sadness, disgust, or even joy—if you breathe smoothly and deeply into the belly while experiencing them, they will diminish and eventually pass rather than lodging deeper into your tissues, only to rear again at a later date. It's when your focus is limited to one aspect of the whole that you lose perspective. Taking the perspective of the whole into consideration and combining that with a nourishing breath serves to metaphorically root us into the soil of life. When we are grounded and nourished, less effort is required to establish, maintain, or reclaim beneficial states of health and happiness. This is true for the individual and for the world around us.

Consider breath as a circle. It comes from outside of us, moves into and through us, and then travels back out to unite with the atmosphere around us again. In doing so, not only does it link us to the world around us, it also links together the four important aspects of who we are, carving a path toward radical relief of stress and glorious good health. Heighten awareness of how you breathe and you step onto the path of wellness and integration. Use the practices outlined in this book, weaving them together as needed, and you will be on your way to mastering your life experiences.

Why not feel, do, and be your best? Learn to breathe, learn to live.

AFTERWORD

If you take care of the minutes, the years
will take care of themselves.
- A Tibetan Saying

I hope that you have enjoyed connecting in a more conscious way with not only your breath but with all the parts of your being as you've navigated the pages of this book. And I hope that you have experienced some beneficial ways to modulate your breathing pattern and your mental concentration in order to influence the activities of your mind and compassionately address life's changing conditions.

Add to that a grateful heart and you will be on your way to living your best life. An attitude of gratitude feeds the soil of our being and strengthens the inner resolve needed to make wise choices. It supports us in seeking positive ways to establish and maintain good health and promote overall well-being. Awareness brings you home. Working with the breath gives you power. These actions minimize stress and enhance relationships, first and foremost with yourself, and then with other important people and experiences in your life. As you weave gratitude, awareness, and willpower together with mindful breathing, your ability to source joy in every moment will increase, and your life will unfold in beautiful ways.

The following blessing expresses my wish for you as you continue down this path.

A Blessing

May your breath be bountiful.
May you breathe with ease and grace.
May the practice of breathing be a soothing and
nourishing experience; one that you choose to
return to again and again.
May you open to and absorb the subtle and
beneficial energies of prana on each level

of your being—body, mind, emotion, and
spirit—as your practice deepens.
As you fill up with life force energy, may
that energy be sensed as good feelings
inside, and may that energy effortlessly spread
out from you into the world around you.
May the art of breathing, as practiced
by you, contribute to fostering
a more peaceful world for
ALL.

Thank you for reading this book. If it has made a difference in your life, please let me and others know that. Spread the word. Spread the love.

Appendix A
General Wellness Tips

As a well spent day brings happy sleep, so a life well spent brings happy death.

-Leonardo Da Vinci

These tips may complement your breathing practice and offer additional support in being the best that you can be and bringing that into all you do. Like breathing, you may already be implementing some of these suggestions. Bringing a sense of mindfulness to them will enhance their health-promoting benefits.

- Adequate hydration keeps your body tissues, including the lungs and diaphragm, fluid and flexible. Drink up to half your body weight in fresh water every day to fuel good health and proper elimination. Only water hydrates adequately.

- Consuming regular meals comprised of whole foods will keep you vital and energized. Take time to enjoy them while minimizing distractions. Food that is lightly cooked in a loving manner is the easiest to digest. Preparing meals at home is a healthier alternative to eating out.
- Engage in moderate aerobic exercise in a serene and regular manner to keep circulation, bones, and muscles strong. Walking, bicycling, and swimming can all be performed in a gentle, health-promoting manner to maintain health.
- Stretch and rest (pause) consciously each day to counteract the demands placed on you throughout the day. Yoga and meditation are great ways to do this.
- Think positive thoughts. Doing so leads to speaking kind words, building positive relationships, and engaging joyfully with health-promoting activities.
- Breathe with awareness. Make time each day to take breaths that are slow and deep. Let them both nourish and become a reflection of the essence of who you really are.

APPENDIX B

A FIVE-WEEK PLAN

Start where you are. Use what you have. Do what you can.

-Arthur Ashe

Week One: **Establishing an Easy Breath**	**Days 1 through 3:** You are learning to breathe effortlessly. Breathe through the nose, if possible, while focusing your mind on the act of breathing. Practice for one to three minutes per session. Only do this as long as you remain comfortable and calm.	**Days 4 through 7:** As comfort grows, add one minute a day, building to a regular practice of five or more minutes of tranquil nose breathing each day. While it is best to practice at the same time and in the same place at least once every day, you are welcome to explore this activity at other times and in other locations as well.

	You are welcome to try this more than once each day, as desired. The goal is to learn to take breaths that are comfortably smooth, deep, and easy. Establish this Easy Breath Practice before moving on.	The Easy Breath Practice should become effortless and harmonious by the end of this week.
Week Two: **The Art of Belly Breathing**	**Days 8 through 10:** Now invite awareness and movement to sink into the belly as you breathe. First, employ the Easy Breath Practice for several minutes (breathing through the nose, if possible). Then place your hands on the lowest part of your abdomen. Invite this area to expand into your hands each time you inhale. Let it move away from your hands every time you exhale. Start with three to five rounds of Belly Breathing Practice and then pause. Notice your experience. Work toward implementing five rounds in one session. Progress further as long you remain stress free throughout the activity.	**Days 11 through 14:** Take a big breath in and sigh it out. Then take three easy breaths through your nose to initiate today's practice. Next, move right into Belly Breathing Practice as you have done the past three days. Add more repetitions to your practice each day if you can remain calm and stress free doing so. Do your best to complete this every day at the same time and in the same place. You may practice at others times as well. Feeling good? Ready to extend the length of time that you practice at any one sitting? You can continue with focused Belly Breathing for as long as you'd like to in any one sitting.

Week Three:	Days 15 through 18:	Days 18 through 21:
Moving inward by listening for the inner sound of the breath or applying a mantra	When your Easy Breath Practice has morphed without effort into Belly Breathing and you are doing this for five to ten minutes or more every day, you are ready to refine your practice. Now is the time to listen for the inner sound of the breath or apply a positive word to each portion of it. Start as you have each day to this point. Turn your awareness inward. Is there a subtle sound that you hear as you listen to your breath? Imagine the sound of *so* as you inhale. Imagine the sound of *hum* as you exhale. Alternatively, apply the syllables of a word to each portion of the breath. Consider using *peaceful*, *joyful*, or *loving*. **Remember:** Cultivate effortless effort. The practice should be comforting.	By now, you should be well established in implementing your daily practice at the same time and in the same place each day. Easy Breath leads into Belly Breathing for the first five to ten minutes. Then extend the length of your practice time by focusing on an inner sound. Not only does this help create a longer practice, it guides the mind to a place of equanimity. The body then gradually learns to abide in equanimity. Allow a mantra to guide your body and mind into a restful state where all that is good can bubble up and permeate your life. **Remember:** At the end of each practice, pause to acknowledge the results before moving on. Gratitude fertilizes intention.

Week Four: **Counting the breath and adjusting the rhythm as needed** **The Mountain Breath**	**Days 22 through 24:** Your daily practice begins at the same time and in the same place each day now, although you may find that you welcome practicing at other times as well. Easy Breath Practice has morphed into Belly Breathing Practice, to which you have added the mental repetition of a sound. This week, you may let go of the sound and instead count the rate at which you are inhaling and exhaling. Do this several times, bringing the length of the inhalation to the same rate as the exhalation to create a balanced breath that is soothing and nourishing. If stress mitigation is your goal, gradually extend the rate at which you exhale over the course of several breaths. While not the way to breathe all the time, letting your exhalation grow longer than your inhalation is a marvelous application in any stressful situation.	**Days 25 through 28:** Substitute The Mountain Breath for counting the breath now. Add a round or two to each day as you progress. **Day 25:** Perhaps three to five rounds of The Mountain Breath are sufficient. **Day 26:** Add an additional one or two more rounds of The Mountain Breath in today. **Day 27:** Consider practicing The Mountain Breath for a full five minutes following five to ten minutes of a Belly Breathing practice today. End by pausing to notice how this breath leaves you feeling. Express gratitude. **Day 28:** Continue as on Day 27, lengthening each part of the practice as is suitable for you.

	Inhaling slightly longer than you exhale may offer an energetic lift. To end, release any formal practice and pause to observe the effects. Express appreciation and then move on. These practices may be used anytime, anywhere to calm, center, and focus you. Let them bring you into a state of equanimity and balance.	Finish by sitting, observing, and absorbing. Express gratitude and move on with comfort in your body, joy in your heart, and peace in your mind. If you would like to explore either of the visualizations in chapter 10 now, please do. Alternatively, substitute one for your breathing practice once a week. It is time to make the process yours. Trust your inner wisdom and enjoy!
Week Five: **Breathe to live via an established daily pranayama practice and the support of creative visualization**	**Congratulations!** You have made your way through the book. I hope you have found that by taking time to breathe with awareness and imagining the positive side of any situation is a pleasant and life-enhancing thing to do. Let these practices support your journey through life. Stay with them. Spend time each day with your practice. Notice how you feel, how you act, and how the world around you and within you adjusts.	Continue. Allow yourself to sit in quiet contemplation at the end of your practice for longer periods of time now. Cherish the connection with your inner world and let the wisdom harbored there become a guiding light, especially when life seems dark. Consider reciting an affirmation, prayer, or intention at the end of your practice each day. This offers a powerful addition to any practice.

	Yay to the benefits of tapping into life force energy! May your experiences be welcomed ones.	Express gratitude for all that is going well in your world, for all you have, and for all you are. May your inner light shine brightly and dazzle the world around you!

Acknowledgements

The light which shines in the eye is

really the light of the heart.

-Rumi

I want to express my profound gratitude for all the people and experiences that have influenced me in some way during the course of my lifetime, for it is you who has led to the writing of this book. My work as a guide to the source of harmony and joy within us, as both a yoga therapist and a holistic wellness educator, has been formed out of my own journey through the ups and downs of life and has taken shape through my interactions with many people, each of whom has influenced my path. It would take many pages to list all of these people.

For the sake of brevity, I am limiting my acknowledgements to three of my principle teachers—Brian Luke Seaward, Sree Devi Bringhi, Hansa Knox—and to the compatriot who introduced me to the magic of yoga during my college years, and subsequently to meditation as a young adult, Kenton Bloom. The confidence each of these masters instilled in me and the depth of conversation and instruction that they have shared with me over the years is much appreciated. Thank you for guiding me back to my Self by doing your own personal work, sharing that generously, and encouraging me to do my own work, too.

I would also like to honor my clients who have shared their physical, mental, emotional, and spiritual struggles and joys with me. I am happy to celebrate the successes you've experienced by learning how to breathe well. Thank you for sharing the journey.

Thank you to Leslie Crosby, Sally Carruthers, Jen Greene, Brownie Harvey, Jo Ann Jones, Brian Luke Seaward, Robert Schram, David Ballard, Kenton Bloom, and Steve Bauhs for your generous review of my manuscript. Thank you also to Paulette K. Kinnes, Larisa Hohenboken, and Melanie

Mulhall for your detailed and professional editing. Thank you, Constance and Kaki Woods and families, for the opportunity to retreat to your mountain home to make final edits to this manuscript before sending it off to be published.

And of course, with the gratitude, love, and all the affection that I hold in my heart, I thank my husband, Todd, who buoys me up with unwavering loyalty and his belief in me, and my children, and my entire extended family. I appreciate the space you all have given me in which to study, write, and pursue my dreams. Without you, my life may have taken a different path. I am grateful for the journey and the breath we share. Thank you for being there.

I also want to acknowledge the wisdom of the life force energy that animates each one of us. Some call it universal love. Others refer to it as the Holy Spirit. At the very least, it is the energy of life that runs through each of us and connects us to something greater than ourselves. Thank you, dear reader, for taking time to explore the possibility of bringing more of that into your life. As you do that, we all grow together. Keep up the good work!

Thank you to Sarah Alexander

for the contribution of your beautiful artwork.

Namaste.

The wholeness and life force energy traveling through me on the breath recognizes the wholeness and life force energy in each and every one of you and in the world around us.

REFERENCES

1) http://drsircus.com/general/breathing-live-longer/
2) http://www.sacred-texts.com/hin/hyp/hyp04.htm
3) https://www.unm.edu/~lkravitz/Article%20folder/Breathing.html
4) https://www.psychologytoday.com/blog/the-neuroscience-mindfulness/201602/the-science-slow-deep-breathing
5) http://www.veroniquemead.com/pns.php
6) http://www.ideafit.com/fitness-library/science-breathing
7) https://www.ncbi.nlm.nih.gov/pubmed/19735239

Referrals to Additional Information

Listen:

- http://www.npr.org/2010/12/06/131734718/just-breathe-body-has-a-built-in-stress-reliever

Read:

- http://www.lifespa.com/15benefits-nosebreathing
- https://www.unm.edu/~lkravitz/Article%20folder/Breathing.html
- The Science of Breathing, Sarah Novotny and Len Kravitz, Ph.D.
- http://www.mountainwisdomyoga.com/articles-to-educate-and-entertain.html (Scan for an article on the vagus nerve)
- http://www.angelfire.com/sc/mrcomeau/respiratory notes.htmlblogs/news/14017853-lifespan-and-breathing-are-they-really-connected
- Breath, Mind, and Consciousness by Harish Johari. Destiny Books, 1989.

Watch:

- https://www.youtube.com/watch?v=P4cmtn0PED4

About The Author

As a certified professional Yoga Therapist and Holistic Stress Management Educator, Sharon competently and lovingly shepherds individuals and groups toward an inner dwelling place where clarity, wholeness, and peace exist. Experienced as a sense of steadiness that is rooted deep within us, the wisdom available to all of us is what allows us to cultivate confidence and joy, and to live life to the fullest, even during tumultuous times.

As a skillful guide, she helps people joyfully unite the pieces of who they are with the roles they play in life, so that they may live their lives feeling more authentic and fulfilled. The people who work with Sharon come to understand the value of taking time to enjoy life as a human being, rather than as a human who is always doing. When not working, Sharon loves to be outdoors and to travel with her family and friends.

For more information visit:

www.MountainWisdomWholisticHealth.com.

To invite Sharon to speak to your group, offer a workshop, or to find out how to work individually with her, you may contact her via email: mountainsmiles@msn.com

A Testimonial To The Author's Work

Humanity is constantly looking for peace, calmness, and relaxation to counter the agitation we find in the world around us. Many times, we try to find this through events outside of ourselves. Sharon, in her program of Mindful Parenting, invited me to pause and breathe, and as a result, I rediscovered the state of peacefulness that exists within me. It takes meditative discipline to touch into inner peace. Yet once we do that, it becomes a habit that releases its benefits unendingly. When that happens, everything around us seems different, better. All that has changed is our relationship with our own self, which has changed for the good. We can only get what we give, and finding the peace that exists within us by consciously tapping into our breath allows us to offer it to the world around us. Work with Sharon. She'll guide you to that inner peace.

Iriana Medina, Mother, Wife and Community Activist

Printed in the United States
By Bookmasters